Praise for 7

"Creativity is an essential skill in business and life, and yet most people are never formally educated in the topic. Patrick has devoted his career to both practicing and teaching creativity in everyday situations. You may be seeking a broad overview, some illuminating examples, a few practical techniques for that project on Monday – or all of the above. If you can't work directly with Patrick, then get this book."

Jason Brown, VP Marketing & Loyalty, eBay Inc

"Patrick Harris provides the manual and the toolkit here which is both easy to follow and to use. Breaking the shackles of uniform thinking and tapping into this reservoir of latent ingenuity may well make the difference between business success and failure. It is therefore an undertaking of great value, and one that is all the more commendable because of its easy to digest layout and prose."

Simon Large, Finlays, Commercial Director

"Patrick changes the way people think about life and the world around them. *The Truth About Creativity* captures who Patrick is—a shaper of ideas and people. This book will draw you in and provide you with a compass to unlock your own creative capabilities."

Andrew Jackson, Ministry of Economic Development, NZ

"Are you a monkey, dolphin, lion or elephant? Do you know the difference between 'urgent' and 'important'? Two fascinating facts I learned from Patrick's wonderful book on creativity. Packed with questions and challenges, this is a must-read for anyone needing to understand creativity."

Ian Ryder, Deputy CEO, British Computer Society

"*The Truth About Creativity* could not be more timely. With extraordinary insight and understanding, Patrick Harris has gently and systematically taken the reader through a process that demonstrates that we all can be creative.

Randolph Kent, PhD, Director, Humanitarian Futures Programme, King's College, London

Thinking creatively is what drives Patrick to get out of bed each morning. *The Truth About Creativity* embodies the thoughts of a man who really enjoys challenging people to think differently. It's great to see his techniques eventually captured on paper in such an easy-to-use and succinct fashion."

Andrew Culpan, Co-Founder Aroxo & former Vice President Strategy
MTV Networks

"A unique perspective on creativity based on Harris's practical experience and his passion for promoting originality and imagination in business. His truths are delivered in a simple structure that is usable and accessible to everyone, making you want to change the way you do things . . . now!"

Jeanette Purcell, Chief Executive, Association of MBAs

"This book debunks the idea that creativity requires total freedom or even anarchy—instead it provides a framework of wonderfully engaging and practical ideas to flex the creativity muscle. Most importantly it doesn't read like an instruction manual, but is more like a very tempting recipe book—and one where you can't wait for the next meal."

Harry Rich, Chief Executive, Enterprise Insight

"Entertaining us with countless stories, riddles and jokes, Patrick Harris expertly leads us out of the proverbial box and into the playground, where he urges us to be bold, to recognise, value and unleash our inherent creativity."

James Goodman, Head of Futures, Forum for the Future

"Patrick clearly illustrates in his book that it is not about to be or not to be creative as a personal characteristic, but it is about how to learn to be more creative as an individual and an organisation."

Willem Manders, Strategy, Change and Assurance Manager, EP
Learning, Shell Exploration and Production

"Patrick is an excellent listener and in many ways personifies 'The Inquisitive Nature'. He takes a rare and wonderfully child-like delight in delving, de-bunking and divulging—and that is one of my definitions of creativity."

Peter Kyle, Chief Executive, The Shakespeare Global Trust

"If Patrick Harris' book on creativity were a cake you'd want to gobble it down in its entirety immediately! It's deliciously excellent."

Camila Batmanghelidjh, Founder, Kids Company

"Patrick's book could do for creativity what Christopher Booker did for story telling with his *Seven Basic Plots*—just with more humour!"

Alex Batchelor, Executive Vice President—Marketing, TomTom

THE TRUTH ABOUT

CREATIVITY

Never forget the 'strength in your story'

Patrick Harris

Prentice Hall
is an imprint of

PEARSON

Harlow, England • London • New York • Boston • San Francisco • Toronto
Sydney • Tokyo • Singapore • Hong Kong • Seoul • Taipei • New Delhi
Cape Town • Madrid • Mexico City • Amsterdam • Munich • Paris • Milan

PEARSON EDUCATION LIMITED

Edinburgh Gate
Harlow CM20 2JE
Tel: +44 (0)1279 623623
Fax: +44 (0)1279 431059
Website: www.pearsoned.co.uk

First published in Great Britain in 2009

ISBN: 978–0–273–72356–1

British Library Cataloguing-in-Publication Data
A catalogue record for this book is available from the British Library

Library of Congress Cataloging-in-Publication Data
Harris, Patrick, 1961-
   The truth about creativity / Patrick Harris.
      p. cm.
   Includes bibliographical references.
   ISBN 978-0-273-72356-1 (pbk.)
 1. Creative ability in business. I. Title.
   HD53.H3745 2009
   658.4'063--dc22

                              2009020714

10 9 8 7 6 5 4 3 2 1
13 12 11 10 09

Typeset in 10/13 pt Meta-LightLF by 3
Printed and bound in Great Britain by Ashford Colour Press Ltd, Gosport

The publisher's policy is to use paper manufactured from sustainable forests.

For Amelia

To me, creativity is simultaneously the most important and least understood aspect of contemporary business. For an occasional, inspired company—it is the lifeblood. I like to think that Orange counts among them. But for the majority, it is a mystery best outsourced to others.

However, understanding, harnessing and investing in creativity are likely to become central to any and all businesses as we move through the twenty-first century. As consumers become more sophisticated, competition more aggressive and regulation more intrusive, the need to find creative solutions, and creative means of serving and interacting with customers, is likely to become acute. Creativity, therefore, must no longer be the sole preserve of the professional creative. It must pervade every division, department and employee.

For that to become true, we have to redefine what we mean by creativity—especially within the context of business. In a harsh commercial setting, creativity could best be defined as synthesis. Every organisation is, to a greater or lesser extent, capable of analysis—deriving trends and tendencies through extrapolation and regression. Only truly creative organisations are capable of synthesis—assimilating and manipulating vast reams of data in a way that results in coherence, insight and the generation of value.

Creativity could also be defined as tension. Too many companies march towards the simplest, most comfortable consensus view without ever challenging the issue. I firmly believe that creativity derives from a healthy—and sometimes painful—tension which forces all concerned to question themselves, their assumptions and everything that has gone before them. Comfortable consensus is the root of all evil.

And as this book very ably demonstrates, creativity is as analytical and systematic as it is free-form and improvised. There is method, process and, undeniably, a clear set of rules.

The book sets out the means by which any organisation can instil, encourage and leverage creativity: not in a contrived way, but in a systemic manner that respects when creativity is needed, how it should be inspired and managed, and perhaps most importantly, when it should reach its conclusion. Unending creativity, with no execution, is as perilous as no creativity at all.

Patrick's unique approach to creativity is extremely powerful and practical. He recognises that creativity should not just be limited to advertising or brand, but should also transcend the whole organisation. It should become a core part of the company's culture. It should inspire and energise—not just employees and customers, but every onlooker.

And to me, that is what makes this book so important. Within a business setting, creativity for its own sake is distracting at best. By contrast, creativity that is bonded to the needs of the business, informed by the preferences of customers, and inspired by the actions of competitors, is potentially transformational.

As the world continues to endure its worst economic downturn since the 1930s, the companies that stand out are those that have creativity at their heart. While the majority bemoan the doom and gloom of reduced consumer spending and gridlocked debt markets, creative companies are finding new routes to market, new types of products and services and new ways of generating income—even as recession bites.

Mindlessly optimistic they are not. They recognise the scale of the world's problems. But their response is to create—to innovate, to change, to act.

Of course, creativity isn't the only answer. But it is a critically important part of the solution—and it is an aptitude that helps to drive every part of a company forward. Moreover, it is an aptitude that can help companies to combat their own, often harmful, reflexes. Cut prices, reduce costs, lay off talented people: the very first things that companies do when the economy takes a dive. Tragically these reflexes are allowed to manifest before creativity is given a chance.

As a result, this book is more important now than ever. It provides a wealth of insights and techniques to help instil creativity throughout the organisation.

Every time you hear another news story that suggests the world is in crisis or the economy is sinking ever faster, I suggest you pick up this book and read—or reread—another of its Truths about creativity. Then think again about how your company should respond to the world around it.

Hans Snook, Founder and former Chief Executive of Orange plc

TRUTH

1

Creativity is yours for the taking

It is a common misconception that only some people are creative. Everyone can, and does, create. True, some people might be better at expressing their creative compositions. Others might have more opportunities to express their flair because they work in a known creative industry. The reality is, however, that everybody is creative.

The reality is that everybody is creative.

Creativity can mean diverse things to different people, so giving it a working definition is important. Here are a few interesting descriptions of creativity from some individuals who know a thing or two about the topic.[1] Each has given a brief response to the question, "What is creativity?" It is a great place to begin:

- "Being informed but not constrained by what went before"—Professor Stephen Heppell
- "Originality; thinking around the subject. Reinterpreting inspirations in an original way"—Zandra Rhodes, CBE, Designer
- "Stimulus that breaks the habit"—Sir Michael Bichard, Rector of the University of the Arts, and Chairman, Design Council
- "Bringing together two or more elements that have never been brought together before, in a combination that triggers something in the observer"—Baroness Susan Greenfield, CBE
- "Thinking outside the box, but in a sphere that really inspires you"—Marissa Mayer, Vice-President Search Products and User Experience, Google
- "The way that life expresses itself; the way that life is formed. It could be new, or an organic repetition"—Antony Gormley, Artist

These thoughts show that creativity is not a lightweight, ancillary topic. It is a serious and vital activity. One that interprets and informs. One that inspires you while it engages others. It is the lifeblood of differentiation at a primary level. The qualities of creativity in these definitions—and many others—are explored throughout this book. At an initial level, however, creativity can be described plainly as a marriage of two or more concepts in a new and interesting way.

Of course, the process of putting two concepts together to get a new answer is available to everyone. It happens all the time. Just look around you. Double-glazed windows. The television remote control. Flexible shower hoses. Everything you can see—even common, everyday items—was once someone's new inspiration from combining two or more ideas.

You can increase your opportunities to marry two or more thoughts together by taking a few simple steps. Use the list below as a recipe for inviting creative moments.

- **Personal strengths**—Refer to these when looking for inspiration or when expressing your creative outcomes. The well-known adage "play to your strengths" applies to creative thinking, as it does for other areas.

> The well-known adage "play to your strengths" applies to creative thinking.

- **Personal shortcomings**—Use these as the means for seeing things from a different point of view. In many ways a perceived weakness can become a realised strength. A poor mathematician is probably a good estimator. A dyslexia sufferer might use influences other than books. Someone with a short attention span can turn to new ideas quickly.

- **Trial and error**—Keep testing possible solutions by trying new combinations of concepts. There are no penalties for trying wrong combinations, but you are instantly rewarded when you find the right one.

- **Best bets**—Take two (or more) independent concepts that work well separately and then marry them together. You may find that they work well together too.

- **Odd bets**—when placing together two (or more) ideas that seem odd or unusual, the combinations may not work well. However, it will spur your thinking about why they are wrong when combined, which can lead to new thought connections.

- **New experiences**—While reflecting on a subject, you could take part in, or observe, new experiences that might lead you to some interesting connections that you had not considered before. A little committed involvement can shed a lot of light.

- **Accident**—Bear in mind that not all creative connections are planned. You cannot plan accidental discoveries, but you should recognise them when they happen and learn from them.

- **Write it down**—Once you have made a connection, take the time to write it down. Think it through to see whether any further insights follow. Revisit your journal of ideas at a later date. Conditions may change and the timing could be just right for one of your ideas to be revitalised and reintroduced at a future time.

Two points are essential for you to remember in your investigation into creativity—namely:

- everyone is creative;
- you have a recipe to invite more creative moments.

Just by bearing these two thoughts in mind, you can reveal more of your own creative potential and clear away mental cobwebs that can stymie innovation. There are degrees of creative talent, of course, just as there are degrees of other skills. Not everyone can be Mozart. However, with the passage of time and experience, your abilities will grow, just as with any skill that you practise regularly. If you spend some time applying the techniques in this book, you might soon find your creative talent blossoming.

TRUTH

2

Creativity is child's play

Imagine you are in a supermarket checkout queue. Nearby, you see an energetic boy, pointing to some sweets and tugging at his mother's arm. With wide eyes, he asks her about buying some sweets, but the answer is "No". Not happy with a simple no, he asks "Why?". She gives her reply, but this too is not enough, so he asks "Why?" again. Sooner or later, one of three things will happen: the mother will buy the sweets; she will explain why he cannot have the sweets; or the mother will become frustrated and say, "You cannot have them, because I say so, that's why."

Finding out about why things are the way they are, and how they work, is a very natural human trait and the building block of creativity. This inquisitive nature is with you from the start. It helps you to make sense of the world and to broaden your knowledge. It can even help to keep you safe from harm. Finding out about things is what creativity is all about. But somewhere, as you grow up, this natural inquisitiveness seems to get suppressed. Why is this?

> Finding out about things is what creativity is all about.

The answer lies partly in systems around you—like education and the workplace—that represent a big slice of your life. It is necessary for these systems to have order and to meet agreed standards, but this sometimes can come at a cost to fostering and retaining creative behaviour. While you are young, education invites you to use and display your skills. Thinking, creating, acting, communicating, playing, sharing, experimentation and physical activities are all part of this experience. Your natural inquisitiveness leads the way. However, once you are older and capable of appreciating different topics, something else happens. Well-meaning parents can sometimes feel a need to structure their children's playtime, stifling independent thinking and removing the need to use initiative. Also at this stage, you are exposed to knowledge about specific subjects, exam goals and lesson plans. This formalisation of the process happens for good reason, but it often lacks a creative flair. Education becomes more about being taught how to do things, rather than thinking for yourself. Learning by thinking for yourself or being encouraged to think for yourself—in the inquisitive manner of a child—gets less attention.

There are, as always, some exceptions. Some teachers help you to learn, rather than teach you set material. You can probably recall a few of the teachers from your past, who stand out from the rest. Many people can. Usually this is because those teachers behaved differently. They challenged you to question and discuss. Then they encouraged you to think for yourself. Memorable teachers like these remind you that creative learning is about taking part.

The workplace, annoyingly, can also suppress your creative behaviour. Organisations are not always adept at inspiring originality in individuals. Rather, organisations are better known for:

- moving a set of people in a particular direction;
- rewarding your ability to follow instructions;
- asking you to fit into a specific profile;
- knowing *what is* rather than asking "*what if?*".

Together, education and the workplace help you to develop a career path. Unfortunately, by the time that you have completed your early education and have started to work, creativity has been, more or less, taught out of you. That natural ability to ask why, like the child in the opening story, has been suppressed. The study of semiotics—linguistic, visual and behavioural signs of society—might suggest that people become anaesthetised to the signals they portray. In other words, what is believed to be an individual's original thought might just be amplification of a popular cultural message. Pablo Picasso said it more simply: "Every child is an artist. The problem is how to remain an artist once he grows up."

The good news is that you can rekindle your creative spirit in a straightforward manner. The key is to re-engage your mind at a creative level—to try to recall those inquisitive games of exploring the world around you. You can do this by:

> You can rekindle your creative spirit in a straightforward manner.

- getting involved—enquiring about and discussing issues;

- thinking things through for yourself;
- being aware of your own views within the wider organisation around you;
- not being afraid to ask what if questions.

Rekindling your creative spirit can happen over the long term, on a day-to-day basis or even as a spontaneous activity. Applying a combination of these three areas is the best way to induce more opportunities. Below are some examples of creative activities that may help you.

- **Long term**—Consider activities that have been on your list of things to do for a long time. These might be taking an art or writing course, trying a new hobby or learning a new skill. Think too about travelling, reading broadly or other activities that take you away from your routine.

- **Short term**—Try taking different routes to your everyday destinations. Small rewards can come from simple things, like window-shopping in different shops on your way to work. Try reading a different newspaper for a few weeks, one that calls you to see the same news through new eyes. Use mind maps that show logical connections between topics instead of taking notes in paragraph form. Excite your senses of taste and smell by trying new flavour combinations.

- **Day to day**—Here, the focus is on setting yourself small spontaneous challenges. They do not have to be strenuous tasks, but they should call into question the normal way that you do things. A good example might be to make a spur-of-the-moment decision to walk through your local park in your business clothes but with bare feet. Setting yourself regular, impromptu challenges is a sure way to reinvigorate creative behaviour.

Above all, keep in mind how children investigate the world around them, in that inquisitive way. Then add this type of discovery to your own activities. You will be amazed at the results.

TRUTH

3

Climb out of your box

The phrase "thinking out of the box" is used liberally and in a number of situations. Teachers ask you to do it. Managers demand it. In spite of the overexposure of the phrase, it is an important attribute of creativity. But what is it that defines your box and what does it mean to think out of it?

Everyone has a box of their own thinking style. This box is a collection of default thinking routes that form the way that you expect things to be. When thinking inside the box, you are comfortable and relaxed about what you might discover. Being inside the box is like being in your thinking home. You are also more mentally constrained when inside your box, which is why it is so important to think outside it.

Puzzles, illusions and brainteasers are good reminders of how people tend to think inside a box. At first, the puzzle proposes a simple game. Then, you realise that you may not be able to complete it. You are lost because traditional thinking will not work but you find it difficult to form new approaches. Finally, you reach a solution, but only by thinking out of the box,

> Being inside the box is like being in your thinking home.

which allows you to see the problem from a completely different angle. Your reward is a solution to the problem, as well as increased confidence and belief in your creative ability. Here is a mind-stretching puzzle for you to think about.

> *A man lives on the tenth floor of a building. Every morning, he takes the lift down to the lobby and leaves the building. In the evening, if there is someone else in the lift, or if it has been raining that day, he goes back to his floor directly, using the lift. Otherwise, he goes to the seventh floor and walks up three flights of stairs to his apartment. Can you explain why?*[1]

You form your safe thinking box in four ways. Understanding these is helpful, as it will better enable you to think outside your box.

- ■ **Tradition**—This is thinking based on years of practical knowledge, proven success and the way things are usually done. There is nothing wrong with tradition, but it is not always helpful when trying to think out of the box and to see a problem from a new perspective.

- **Linear thinking**—This form of thinking assumes that what happened before will happen again, and at the same pace. Change, of course, is not always linear. Change can occur in both an evolutionary and a revolutionary fashion. Evolutionary change is predictable and foreseeable. Revolutionary change is much more disruptive. It breaks the mould of what went before and can alter entire systems overnight. Paper, the printing press, steamships, Henry Ford's mass production methods of the 1900s and the introduction of the contraceptive pill in the 1960s are all examples of revolutionary changes through history.

- **Limited experience**—The experiences that you have been a part of or have witnessed form the basis for categorising new events. This is a wonderful trait for developing your memory and for recalling specific events. What this process does not do, though, is to help you attach unlike, or different, items together.

- **Lifespan thinking**—This describes thinking that is constrained by the time that you have spent on the planet. It can be difficult for you to consider the world without placing yourself inside it.

Thinking out of the box requires you to relax these "in the box" modes and to display other traits. Thinking out of the box is a mental state where you:

- are happy to discard convention;
- keep an open mind about the problem;
- are not afraid to try new approaches;
- investigate new areas;
- build on the ideas and thoughts of other people.

Moving out of the box occurs when you step away from the usual ways of solving problems. You leave behind the thinking traps of tradition, linear thinking, limited experience and lifespan thinking. View it as a dam that you construct to direct your flow of thoughts in new directions. One way to achieve an out-of-the-box mental state is to be stimulated into thinking differently with an exercise—such as role play. To illustrate, place yourself in the lead role in the following story for a moment.

Imagine that you are sitting in a library. The sum told knowledge of human existence is at your fingertips. This place is the academic centre of the universe, global leader in innovation and an asset that befits the richest country in the world. Success has brought people from every corner of the globe to compete in global trading markets. Your country has been the powerhouse of the world economy for more than two generations. The grain and oil that it produces has brought stability and prosperity to the world. Internationally, country has not fought country for over fifty years. Outside of this developed area is another world, where people do not have access to food and clean water. These people must look upon the imposing culture, immense wealth and arrogant stance of your world with envy or disdain.

You complete your work. Oil prices have risen 10 per cent in three months. If they continue at this rate, there will be world recession, because the economy is heavily reliant on this basic commodity.

Where do you think you are? Rather, when do you think you are? London in 1860? New York in 1980? Beijing in 2020? Actually, you are in Alexandria in 250 BC. Britain was circumnavigated for the first time just fifty years earlier. Jesus Christ has not been born. The oil prices you are studying are not crude, but olive.[2]

Seeing a problem from another angle helps you to challenge convention. If you are helping a team of people to use out-of-the-box thinking for a longer period, several exercises spaced throughout the day are a good idea. Having the services of an experienced facilitator can be helpful too.

Seeing a problem from another angle helps you to challenge convention.

More than anything, getting out of the box involves leaving conventional thinking behind, asking what if questions and then openly exploring the ideas that follow.

TRUTH

4

Map your journey before you explore

It is important to know where you want to go—and why—before you creatively explore. It is too easy sometimes to start applying your creative tools to a problem area, before really thinking through the reasoning behind the existence of the problem.

Organisations regularly face weighty, difficult issues. It is also fair to say that at any given point in time, there are a number of talented, well-meaning people inside those organisations who are trying to find solutions to wrong problems. They stand a chance of misdiagnosing the situation by not first appreciating the issue. Sadly, the pressures and systems of offices can often lead to an approach of shoot first and ask questions later.

Spending a little time, thought and energy beforehand can save a lot of anguish in the long run. Devoting this reflective time at the outset is one of the most important tasks to go through *before* you start imaginative problem-solving. Clarity at the outset is worth the effort you invest. Follow these three easy steps to map your journey.

> Clarity at the outset is worth the effort you invest.

1. Avoid assumptions.
2. Set your destination.
3. Know when you have arrived.

Step 1—Avoid assumptions

Assumptions can be explanative, welcome tools. For instance, they can be used to underwrite intentions such as, "We will achieve x within six months, as long as y remains available to us." Often, however, assumptions are erroneously used as substitutes for factual data. People assume what will work, what will be desirable, what customers will like, what decision-makers want to hear and much more. To make matters worse, more assumptions are often built on the back of the initial supposition. This is all fine as long as the assumptions made are correct. But who is to know?

The best approach is to avoid making glaring assumptions without some basis for doing so. There will be times when you will need to step out on a limb, however. When you do, qualify your view with the best information you can locate, given the time and resources allowed. Also, be prepared to knock your assumptions off their pedestal and discard them when contrary conclusions are shown to be evident. Don't be caught defending the indefensible.

Step 2—Set your destination

It is no good just taking the direction of others and meandering along behind them. For a start, it might hamper your own creative explorations. Additionally, you might find that what you are being creative about is not focused in the right area.

Consider a frozen pond. You are afraid to venture out because the ice may be too thin at this time of year. So you wait. With time, someone else comes along and walks across the pond. Soon more people turn up and walk across the ice. Is the ice any less hazardous because people have crossed it? Has anything significant changed to make you want to walk across? Before you answer, substitute the frozen pond with the bursting of the dotcom investment bubble in 2000, or the economic crash following sub prime lending in 2008. Remember the rush of traders that were flooding into these areas in advance of the crashes? What was their reasoning, other than the fact that "the ice" looked OK, given that no one had fallen through yet?

If you fail to set your own direction for your creative attempts, you could find yourself outmanoeuvred or out of step. For example, you could be making a better ice skate for a frozen pond, while all around you others are making dinghies because they have discovered that the ice has started to melt.

State what you want to do, where you want to go and how you want to get there. Appreciate when different creative approaches have their merits. Explore new areas and build on existing ideas. Dismantle orthodoxy that inhibits you and draw synthesis from the analysis

> Have a plan, then put it into practice.

that you apply. Have a plan, then put it into practice. Having a plan doesn't stop you from deviating later, if needs be. What a plan does is to highlight an expected or preferred route and to focus your attention on progress made and goals to come.

Step 3—Know when you have arrived

The start of a project is usually an exciting time. Spirits are high, as are expectations, and everyone looks towards a successful outcome. The question is, does everyone share the same concept of success? The answer is probably not, if you have not spelled it out clearly. Think about what you want to achieve. Will you focus on overall impact achieved or on specific outcomes? Will you accomplish something on a grand scale or demonstrate success with a small prototype? Do you hope to invoke a decision? Create a movement? Set an example? Whatever your plans for success may be, spell them out clearly and be prepared to demonstrate the resulting success when it happens.

Think also about what success would feel like. Do you envisage everyone pulling together in the same direction as a successful outcome? Would success be implementing a solution that finally puts an age-old topic to rest—once and for all? Or maybe your version of success is about completeness and knowing that every angle has been reviewed. How would your colleagues or your manager describe the attributes of a successful outcome?

How you define your end point is up to you. The key thing is to know what your destination might look like, so that you can recognise it when you arrive.

Mapping your creative journey is no different from making other travel plans. You will want to know where you are going and how you will get there. All that you need to change are the vehicles that you use.

TRUTH

5

Give creativity a guide

Guiding your creative actions with a few principles—before exploring— will ensure that you know where you want to go and how you are going to get there. You will save valuable time and apply greater clarity over the long run. With this much at stake, understanding *how* to guide your creative work is worth investigating more closely.

Your creative activities will be subject to unplanned events. It is a fact of life that not everything will be carefully laid out and prepared in advance. Yet, even within shifting situations, there is often a consistency in how you tend to behave. This consistency of behaviour comes from your inherent personal characteristics and your customary reactions in times of uncertainty—your guiding principles. Guiding principles help you to manage your day-to-day tasks in a coherent manner so that you can get on with the important role of being creative.

Think of a fire alarm suddenly going off in a busy space. Some people would look after themselves first. Others might rescue less able people. Some might contact emergency services while others might attempt to save their belongings. The point is that everyone would respond to the emergency. Yet no one would have the time to read a reference manual, write a strategy or compare and contrast the options available. They would just act. However, each person would act in accord with their core behaviours—their guiding principles.

The example illustrates how everyone has guiding principles. They are the ideal tool for giving you clarity inside embryonic,

Everyone has guiding principles.

creative situations. Unfortunately, not everyone is aware of their principles. Furthermore, despite their usefulness, guiding principles can be taken for granted. Because they are innate,[1] people don't always take the time to appreciate them fully. Most people think more about the weekly shopping list than they do about what constitutes their core behaviour.

Understanding your guiding principles

Guiding principles are broad statements that are malleable enough for you to interpret in specific circumstances of creative activity. Here are some examples of what they could look like:

- "Be true to self."
- "Form follows function."
- "Honesty is the best policy."
- "That which does not destroy me makes me stronger."

It is critical that your set of principles conveys significant meaning for you. For example, the phrase "be true to self" is a paraphrase from Shakespeare's *Hamlet*, but perhaps you first heard it from a friend helping you to make a crucial decision at a particular time.

Being able to appreciate and express your principles is a thought-stimulating but straightforward exercise. Here is one approach. Before you launch into your next creative programme, take some time to look for consistencies in your behaviour and ask yourself why these are in place. When looking, you might find some of the following questions to be helpful:

- What are your favourite books? Favourite authors? Why?
- Which people from history do you most admire? Which traits?
- Which are your favourite movies? Favourite directors?
- How would the people closest to you describe you in just one or two words? (Consider your parents, best friend, favourite teacher, partner, etc.)
- What is the earliest memory you can recall?
- What are the most memorable/important parental instructions you can recall?
- Do you have any maxims that you find yourself repeating regularly?

Try to answer these, or your own, similar questions that provide personal glimpses of your preferred way of doing things. Your answers will be phrases that describe your key behaviours. Only a small number of these behaviours—maybe six or fewer—exist at a high enough level to represent your guiding principles. Cull your list to reach a resulting few statements—strong, personal beliefs that you regularly depend on. These are your guiding principles. They are ideal to refer to as a guide when you are immersed in creative situations, where key decisions are required and when you are having to adapt to uncertain circumstances.

Using guiding principles

Being aware of your guiding principles will give you more time to explore new areas, look for compatible circumstances that "fit" with your way of doing things and get on with the task of creatively solving problems.

A friend once shared how a principle from his approach to fishing worked into his life. If he felt that he was not catching enough, he would happily change location while out fishing. His view was, "I can always come back here and carry on catching at the same rate as before." He found himself applying this principle elsewhere in his life. One example concerned his outlook at work, giving him the confidence to look for more exciting opportunities.

When given the chance to problem-solve creatively, it is tempting to jump in with eagerness and at a moment's notice. A more discerning approach, however, is to consider the principles that you regularly rely on and then use these to guide your creative actions. The result will be greater consistency in your activities, more time to be creative and more reward from working in your preferred way when addressing a project. *What you want, more time to do it, in the style that suits you.* This is the importance of knowing your principles.

> Consider the principles that you regularly rely on and then use these to guide your creative actions.

TRUTH

6

Tune in to turn creativity on

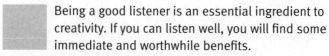 Being a good listener is an essential ingredient to creativity. If you can listen well, you will find some immediate and worthwhile benefits.

- You will better understand the needs to be addressed.
- You will set off in the right direction when creatively exploring.

- You will be sought out when others want to share ideas because you will gain a reputation for being a good listener.

Together, these benefits will give you the chance to be exposed to more creative opportunities and to do more with this information.

The difficulty is that listening well can be hard to do. It is a skill just like golf or cooking, where practising good technique can

Listening well can be hard to do.

improve your abilities. If your listening skills are not at their best, then you will miss out on opportunities, will make fewer interesting thought connections and might even waste time trying to solve some of the wrong issues.

It is helpful first to look at three difficulties that get in the way of good listening. These are warning signs to look out for.

Listening conditionally is the first difficulty. You might tend to hear what you want to hear or are conditioned to hear. This is because you more readily hear thoughts that are compatible with your own views. Conditional listening can vary enormously, depending on your familiarity with a topic and your faith in a speaker. Conditional listening also happens because you have your own framework of personal experiences. You use your past experiences to catalogue new information, similar to a filing system. People regularly listen conditionally—for example, during meetings. Just ask five people leaving a meeting for a summary and you are likely to get five different answers.

A second difficulty when you are listening is a **loss of control from being unable to communicate your own needs**. Speakers hold the keys to control. Listeners have to wait for their turn. This may sound obvious, but it is important to realise the implications of this one-way operation. When you are unable to express your needs, you can feel vulnerable and exposed. If the inability to express your needs continues, you can reach an uncomfortable, or even frustrated, state. You are stirred to respond but cannot because you are busy listening. The feelings of vulnerability, exposure, discomfort and frustration begin to creep in and compete with your ability to listen well.

As a speaker, others are waiting and watching you. You can sense levels of agreement (or not) from the body positions and responses of others. For a listener, the role is reversed. Listeners are busy thinking about what they might say when the opportunity arises and how they might regain control of the conversation. Ultimately, the loss of control that you feel as a listener causes you to plan your next steps before the speaker has finished. The time that you spend thinking about the views that you want to express is time that is not spent listening well.

The third difficulty is **the rate at which listening happens**. Basically, you hear—and others speak—at a slower rate than you can think. Your mind can quite easily look for and absorb lots of other material—related or not—when you are trying to listen. When you say to someone that they "have your undivided attention", the reality is that this is probably not true.

This difficulty is made more apparent when there are lots of distractions present. Passive distractions are things like background or ambient noise—for example, others talking nearby or a whirring ceiling fan. However, as a listener, you can also actively *seek* distractions, by occupying your mind with other activities. This is particularly true if you are not overly interested in the topic.

There is a subtle difference, however, between a distraction that inhibits listening and a purposeful intervention to improve it. Some studies have suggested that when you listen and, at the same time, use your hands to explore the topic, more synapses are created in the brain. This is not so unusual when you recall that your brain is an organ that grows through perception and interaction. More synapses means that more of the brain is engaged, more mental connections are forming and that you might actually be listening better than someone who is not using their hands. Model building and sketching are good examples of this in practice.

Knowing about these three listening difficulties is helpful, because you can now show greater empathy for those listening to you. You know that they will be conditionally categorising your words, forming what they want to say and being distracted. Being aware of the potential pitfalls can make you a better communicator.

Being aware of the potential pitfalls can make you a better communicator.

Tactically, there are a number of approaches that can improve your ability to listen well.

- **Ask questions**—This can add clarity and shows your interest in what the speaker is saying.

- **Seek confirmation**—To ensure that you have heard correctly or to have key points reiterated.

- **Delay your response**—Waiting just a few seconds can be enough to ensure that everything the speaker wants to say has been said. You will be less likely to try to regain control of the conversation too early.

- **Minimise distractions**—You can improve your ability to focus by removing any obvious distractions in advance. If you find that a distraction arises during a conversation, ask whether you can remove it. Explain to the speaker that you want to do this in order to hear them better.

- **Empathise**—Try to appreciate the speaker's point of view. It is still possible to show your respect, even if you disagree.

The most obvious improvement that you as a listener can put in place is to get the speaker to talk more. While they are talking, you know that they are not feeling the difficulties of listening. They are instead communicating their needs. Meanwhile, you will be establishing a strong creative base of hearing the needs of others, setting off in the right direction and gaining a reputation as a good listener.

TRUTH

7

Creativity is a way of thinking

At its core, creativity is a way of thinking and a way of seeing things. It is inclusive, inquisitive and expansive. Inclusive because you seek the involvement and input of others. Inquisitive because you look for answers to *what if*, *how* and *why*. Expansive due to the variety of options considered.

Creativity is a thought system, just as logic and scientific method are systems. It allows you to see an issue from different angles. Yet creativity does not exist as a universally agreed, fully documented process. This is a good thing because it preserves the innocence of looking at things with a fresh perspective.

> Creativity is a thought system, just as logic and scientific method are systems.

Organisations apply creative thinking in new product development and start-up environments. It can also complement other thinking styles. Evidence gathered by logic and scientific method, for instance, might still need a creative focus afterwards to construct a fitting solution. Regardless, you will find some common ground in all descriptions of creative thinking. First, it is iterative, not linear. It is a continuous pattern of expanding, contracting and testing. Second, any creative thinking activity will address at least four key questions:

1.   What need is being addressed and for whom?
2.   Can you visualise the concept?
3.   Why is the situation like this?
4.   What are the options?

What need is being addressed and for whom? The basis of most creative investigations is a clear articulation of what need is being served, why it is there and who will benefit from addressing it. When you outline a problem from an end-user perspective, you are targeting your focus appropriately. By adding to this a creative way of thinking, you look for a system of causes and effects. Together these approaches ensure that the right problem is being addressed and that implications resulting from any proposed solutions are understood.

The iBOT, for example, is a wheelchair that climbs kerbs and stairs, as well as raising riders to standing height. Both are solutions to long-term complaints from wheelchair users. The thinking focused on the need—and the solution was a new, creative one.[1]

Can you visualise the concept? A creative process can begin with the expression of a grand vision, uniting people to a cause. One of the most recognised grand visions of recent times was President Kennedy's goal that inspired the space race—to put a man on the moon by the end of the decade and bring him back safely.

Visualisations of possible solutions can also inspire others. The 1996 winning consortium[2] in London's Millennium Bridge design inspired the competition organisers and the public with a concept of a *blade of light*. J.K. Rowling, in her website biography, mentions how helpful (and lucky) it was that when the concept of Harry Potter entered her mind, she was stuck on a train for four hours. With no pencil and paper, she sat and mentally developed her vision for the whole magical world she would go on to create.

You, as a visionary, often hold the intricate details of how an entire concept might develop. If this cannot be articulated, an underpinning ideology can be shared instead. The concept of Swatch watches is an example of setting out an ideology (to rewrite the rules of watch ownership), without necessarily knowing a precise solution.

Why is the situation like this?
This question is about investigation, insights and ideas. This aspect of a creative way of thinking looks for footholds of inspiration that have the potential to be developed further. Investigation is for making sense of the present environment. Insights are beginnings that could lead to ideas. Ideas are formed from mentally rubbing two or more thoughts together and expressing what that combination might produce. Throughout this phase of creative thinking, you are focused on establishing a foundation of thoughts. Always building on your investigations, insights and ideas.

> Insights are beginnings that could lead to ideas.

What are the options? Here, alternatives are generated that could address the issue. The options are tested and considered against expectations and against the original stated need. Prototypes can help to trial alternatives and to refine eventual solutions. This aspect of creative thinking is centred on generating more complete ideas, evaluating them and receiving feedback. Sometimes, you may need to exaggerate a point to help people to see options.

For example, the board at a company I worked with asked for guidance in leading a knowledge-sharing programme. They were convinced that an electronic document-sharing system was the answer. I was less sure. At one update meeting, I opted not to use the slide presentation format. Instead, and to their astonishment, I asked the board to juggle, giving them each a set of juggling balls with instructions. Ten minutes later I stopped them in the midst of their fun. I explained that while they were industrious in solving the juggling problem, none of them had used the tool supplied (the instructions). Some of them learnt by asking a colleague (culture). Some of them stood facing a wall (process). Some of them moved chairs away, or used a space with a higher ceiling (environment).

I compared the juggling instructions to an electronic document-sharing system. Both are tools. I said that not everyone in the organisation would use the document system by default, just as the board didn't use the instructions given. I told them that they were forcing a preconceived solution on to a problem that had not been creatively explored. In that moment, their support was won. Eventually they invested in a more holistic knowledge sharing programme centring on culture, process, environment and tools.

Creativity as a way of thinking is summarised in the checklist below:

- It is all about inclusion. No one is superhuman or super smart.
- Retain your inquisitiveness and ask questions.
- Build on ideas and on conversations. There are no negatives.
- If at first you don't succeed, try and try again.
- Lay out your vision and how it might be fulfilled.
- Make sure that end users are at the heart of your needs.
- Test your alternatives and look for feedback.

Use this list to remind you of ways to think when you are not convinced of the preconceived solutions that someone else has thrust upon you, or when you need to get your creative thoughts flowing.

TRUTH

8

Make time for creativity

Making time to be creative is no different from making time for anything else. If you have the free space in your diary, fine. If you don't, then something else has to go.

This is basic time management. By managing your time well, you will maximise your efficiency across a spectrum of areas, including creativity. What a waste it would be, for instance, if you were to find yourself having some free time to apply your imagination to a problem, but then discovered that you had left some crucial information at the office. This sort of thing happens often. The issue is a logical one, of forgetfulness or inattention. It is logic that fails you but creativity that suffers. Thankfully you can address this problem with some basic tools like list-making and note-taking and by applying some measured prioritisation.

One solid example is making a **things-to-do list**. Knowing the best time for you to build your list can be important. For instance, you might choose to start your day by writing out a plan of activities. Alternatively, you might enjoy writing it out at the end of the day to clear your head and to gain a mental headstart on

> A things-to-do list is a simple but very effective way to generate more creative time for you.

the following day's activities. In any case, constructing a things-to-do list is a simple but very effective way to generate more creative time for you. Find the approach that works best for you and be prepared to adapt and improve it over time.

Years ago, a friend asked me whether my things-to-do list contained important or urgent tasks. I said that I wasn't sure. He explained that important tasks were those I really wanted or needed to do and urgent tasks were those that were pressing for attention. Urgent, he said, might be things like emails to address or a meeting to attend. Using his definition, important tasks could be completely different, like seeing my son's sports match or looking into an arts course. He said that my things-to-do list should contain both. Since that day, my things-to-do lists have always had an indication of importance (high, medium, low) and urgency (priority 1, 2 or 3) against each task. It helps to ensure that both areas receive sufficient attention.

Note-taking is another area that can build creative time for you.

Taking notes helps you to confirm your thoughts as you write, while providing a permanent record to refer to later on. Try sketching too. At a meeting, sketch the layout of the table, windows and the seating position of others. Jot down comments to remind you of attributes of the people present. You can also paste items into your notes, such as the agenda, emails, photos and other related material. This descriptive record might help you to recall specific items or the overall tone of the conversations. As a result of your note-taking efforts, you will have a richer account of what was said—and meant.

Lists and notes allow you to assign priority to tasks that you are aiming to complete. What do you want to accomplish at home? In your relationships? At work? In your dreams? By capturing and referring to your priorities, you will maintain a better creative focus on the things that really matter to you. Below is a popular story circulated on the internet about filling your life completely.[1]

> By capturing and referring to your priorities, you will maintain a better creative focus.

A professor stood before his philosophy class and had some items in front of him. When the class began, wordlessly, he picked up a very large and empty mayonnaise jar and proceeded to fill it with golf balls. He then asked the students if the jar was full. They agreed that it was. So the professor then picked up a box of pebbles and poured them into the jar. He shook the jar lightly. The pebbles rolled into the open areas between the golf balls. He then asked the students again if the jar was full. They agreed it was.

The professor next picked up a box of sand and poured it into the jar. Of course, the sand filled up everything else. He asked once more if the jar was full. The students responded with a unanimous, "yes".

The professor then produced two cans of beer from under the table and poured the entire contents into the jar, effectively filling the empty spaces between the sand. The students laughed. "Now," said the professor, as the laughter subsided, "I want you to recognize that this jar represents your life. The golf balls are the important things—your family, your health, your children, your friends, your favourite passions—things that if everything else was lost and only they remained, your life would still be full. The pebbles are the other things that matter like your job, your house or your car. The sand is everything else—the small stuff."

"If you put the sand into the jar first," he continued, "there is no room for the pebbles or the golf balls. The same goes for life. If you spend all your time and energy on the small stuff, you will never have room for the things that are important to you. Pay attention to the things that are critical to your happiness. Play with your children. Take time to get medical checkups. Take your partner out to dinner. Play another 18. There will always be time to clean the house, and fix the disposal. Take care of the golf balls first, the things that really matter. Set your priorities. The rest is just sand."

One of the students raised her hand and inquired what the beer represented. The professor smiled and replied, "I'm glad you asked. It just goes to show you that no matter how full your life may seem, there's always room for a couple of beers."

Creativity is not hard to put into your life; there are simple, logical tools you can use to allow it to flourish. Just be sure that you focus on the right things at the right time and make sure that the small stuff—the sand—does not get in the way.

TRUTH

9

Don't stop at the first idea

Being creative means not stopping at the first idea that comes along. The first idea is really only a starting point. You might return to it later or build variations on it, but don't be tempted to quit at your first insight. First ideas are critical to begin with, for getting a flow of thoughts, but they tend to have undesirable traits about them. The first idea is likely to be apparent—the thought that everyone else will share. It might have resonance with other people but it won't be unique. The first idea will probably only represent an incremental change. Incremental change can be part of the solution, but a creative activity should explore significant step changes and radical thoughts as well. By thinking beyond the first idea, you are free to explore a number of ways to achieve your desired impact.

The following story highlights the limitations that can accompany first ideas. Some friends of mine were talking about maintaining UK sporting excellence. The first idea presented would be to identify and invest in a few new Olympic sports. It was immediately accepted by everyone. Why not? It was obvious, it seemed logical and it resonated well. But no other options were even considered, despite much more talking. What about the option of investing in specific athletes, instead of sports? This would be in keeping with the mentality of individuals rising to meet their challenges.

A second solution might be to change the way medal tables are presented. For instance, why not promote a table stating the number of medals won, relative to size of the Olympic team competing? Still another solution might be to invest in non-Olympic sports instead. This solution asks about the intent of the question. Is Olympic medal success seen as a link to promoting wider participation in sport? If so, are there other ways to achieve greater sports participation in the general population?

One great approach to generating a number of ideas is to apply different viewpoints. Now, unless you have the facilities to invite a few thousand friends over for a chat, you will need other ways to

One great approach to generating a number of ideas is to apply different viewpoints.

represent a large number of views. Viewing lenses may be just what you need. A viewing lens is simply you trying to see the issue from the perspective of another group. Groups to consider include customers, shareholders, partners, management, suppliers and even competitors. Anyone that you regard to be a stakeholder in the topic is worth embracing.

Other viewing lenses include fringe groups, embedded members of the current establishment (who might be opposed to new ideas) and groups who have no exposure to the topic at all. For example, it was a fringe group of surfers in the 1950s and 1960s who invented skateboarding, just by looking for ways to mimic surfing when not on the water. Viewing lenses can also be particular values that you want to see emphasised.

Great worth was given to seeing things through five brand values during my time at mobile phone company Orange.[1] Typically, meetings in those early years would reach a seemingly suitable conclusion—that is, until someone would ask about the values. How was the proposed solution representative of one or more of the values? If there was consistency, great. If not, then the whole team went back to the drawing board. Viewing items through the lenses of the brand values meant that everything eventually had a consistent Orange look and feel about it, as well as having a creative outcome.

You can gather first-hand perspectives of other groups from interviews, questionnaires, peer review, focus groups or other sampling methods. However, gathering views is not necessarily where your creativity comes into play. This happens by studying and discussing these other perspectives and drawing inferences afterwards.

You can aid interpretation of your perspectives through role play— wearing the hats of other groups that you see as important. When acting in this mode, ask questions that your chosen groups would be concerned about:

- Is the issue evident and relevant to each group?
- Do they each share the same need as you?
- From their perspective, what would a good solution look like?
- Who are the winners in a given solution? Who are the losers?

If you are working with others, you can put together a game where everyone occupies a role for a different key group. Each player, in turn, acts out events in response to a given situation. Imagine the value of reviewing ideas through the eyes of your customers and shareholders, as well as representatives from several of your organisation's departments—in the same room and at the same time. This is what role play can achieve. It will provide you with insight into relationships between different groups, some views on the potential impact of a given solution and a greater number of ideas to consider.

There are a few things to bear in mind when generating many ideas. First, it is not good to overevaluate them in the early stages. Try to express ideas, not assess them.

Second, listen to others as they state their ideas and then build on these concepts. Third, pay attention to the ideas that are "sticky". Sticky

> Try to express ideas, not assess them.

ideas are ones that are easily recalled and that cleverly address a clear need. They are the ones that cause you to nod in agreement when they are voiced. Sticky ideas are in your memory, even much later, when most of the other concepts have long been forgotten. Lastly, you should avoid negative expressions. Most of these are well known to you, because businesses are rife with them:

- "The boss won't like it. He never does."
- "We've been there and done that."
- "I can't see it happening here."

Instead, try to encourage ideas by giving some positive reinforcement. Acknowledging the idea of someone else and then building on it with some of your own thoughts is all that is needed. It will encourage a greater number of ideas to be put forward and huge diversity in the way that these ideas are explored and expanded. Once you are generating more ideas with greater diversity and you are seeing things through the lenses of important groups, you are almost certainly destined for a creative outcome.

TRUTH

10

Rules are there to be challenged

Sometimes, you can—and maybe should—challenge the rules that are around you. Overcoming conventional thinking and questioning the status quo is part of being creative. Besides, the rules that you are facing could have come from out-of-date systems or people who have now moved on. Challenging the rules and the accepted view helps you to escape from the confines of limited thinking and opens the door to possibilities.

Here are four types of situation where you may find it particularly beneficial to challenge the rules and the accepted thinking.

- Some rules look to be outdated or inconsistent with the current need.
- You sense the presence of 'taboo' topics.
- You suspect that some tasks are seen as just too hard to tackle.
- You hear the phrase "the way that things are done around here".

Outdated, or inconsistent, rules can be obvious and are usually begging for attention, but they often go unchecked because they are left for someone else to address. They are regularly discussed in the lunchroom or by the coffee machine. These rules are often about the situations that everyone sees as redundant or laughable.

Consider this story told by a friend of mine about how dreadfully outdated a rule can become. In London after the Second World War, bicycles were used extensively due to their low cost and because of fuel shortages. One car park, overcrowded with bicycles, instituted a signing-in system. Only signed-in owners could park their bikes and the system worked wonderfully. About 40 years later, and after many changes in fuel prices and transport development, people were still riding their bicycles into work and still signing in at the security desk. One day, one of the cyclists, feeling reflective, asked why it was necessary to sign in. The person on duty did not know why and agreed to see what would happen if everyone stopped. The result? Immediately, the cyclists could enter hassle-free, the signing-in book vanished and the morning security team found something a little more meaningful to do at that time of day.

Taboo, or sacred cow, topics exist because of some particularly strong views from before. Taboo topics lie unaddressed because no one really believes that any suggested

Taboo items are seen as untouchable.

changes will be supported. Taboo items are seen as untouchable. These are the reasons why you should look at them carefully and question their relevance.

A tricky taboo topic emerged when I worked with Shakespeare's Globe, the iconic theatre structure on London's Bankside.[1] From the start, it was easy to see that entering the site was less glamorous than could be expected. Two entrances were used, but the primary route was ignored. Worse, the primary route is a spectacular entrance through wrought iron gates that face the River Thames and its throngs of strolling visitors. The entrance had been closed because site operational staff were afraid that the premises would be exposed to graffiti, unscrupulous visitors and unhelpful traffic flow. Opening the gates was a taboo topic—one that no one believed could be challenged. So, taking a gamble, I opened the gates one day. Staff condemned and praised the action in equal numbers. Visitors, however, walked into the place as naturally as if they had been doing it for years.

Afterwards, a trial opening period was held, proving that the open gates attracted more people. The result is that the gates are now open each year during the key visitor seasons. The previous ten years of worries—vandalism, revenue and traffic flow—were solved too, just by adding a short piece of red barrier rope and moving a security desk by a few feet.

Neglected tasks that are seen as **too hard to tackle** may not be quite as obvious as outdated rules or taboo topics. Items that are too hard to tackle do not always receive regular attention because no one sees the benefit of taking charge. This is because a positive result is seen as unlikely, either for the issue addressed or the person who tackles it. Neglected tasks often need to be broken down into the underlying causes and then into digestible elements that can be addressed. This ensures that each element is seen in a new light, that solving them piece by piece represents progress and that there will be tangible benefits to come. Good communication about this new approach to solving the issue is important throughout the task.

Items that fall under the heading of **"the way things are done around here"** are always worth questioning. Sometimes "the way things are done" is almost legendary and outlives the original intent of that approach.

Items that fall under the heading of "the way things are done around here" are always worth questioning.

A friend enjoys recounting the time that he decided to cancel his home milk deliveries. It happened after he saw a food store's home delivery vehicle, dramatically framed by a bright sunrise, overtaking a sluggish milk float.[2] He realised immediately that the cart represented the way that things had been done for years and that the home delivery vehicle was a vivid example of thinking through the issue with new clarity.

There is much to be gained by putting into play the four rule-challenging situations described above.

■ You test the resolve of the people involved.

■ You identify the limits of the issue and potential solutions.

■ You overcome barriers to thought.

■ You qualify the broader understanding of the issue and its challenges.

■ You create new possibilities.

■ You try new approaches.

■ You gain knowledge and share this with others.

■ You question accepted assumptions and expected outcomes.

When rule challenging, bear in mind the following four tips for success.

■ Know the associated risks and how you will alleviate these.

■ Look for help from those who are not afraid to rock the boat a little.

■ Be aware of your own conventions and biases.

■ Be prepared to follow through when a solution is found.

By knowing when to challenge rules, how you might benefit and what to be aware of along the way, you will be better equipped to tackle some thorny issues. More importantly, you might uncover a creative solution for a problem that has been lingering in your organisation for years.

TRUTH

11

It ain't what you say, it's the way that you say it

Having creative ideas is one thing. Sharing your thoughts with a variety of people is quite another matter. Communicating effectively is crucial in order for you to convert your ideas into reality. You will increase your opportunity for creative success by giving your audience what *you* want to say, in the way that *they* want to receive it.

There are two hurdles that could get in your way when voicing your ideas. The first is, *how much do they want to hear it?* You could be facing resistance or competing agendas—knowingly or not. Be articulate and convincing about the key benefits of your idea. Make sure that your story addresses the concerns of the audience members. The more clear and convincing you can be, the more bullet-proof your idea becomes.

The second hurdle you face is, *how well have they heard you?* To communicate effectively—even with wholly willing audiences—you will need to be clear, complete and concise. As soon as you share an idea, it is subjected to interpretation and retelling. These are very welcome activities that spread the good news about your idea. But it is important that other versions of your story are in keeping with your original intent. Make sure that you communicate your idea completely and in a way that can be easily remembered.

> The more clear and convincing you can be, the more bullet-proof your idea becomes.

Tips for communicating creative thoughts

Below are a few areas of focus that will help you to share your ideas with clarity.

- Know when, how and where to communicate.
- Consider the overall clarity of your message.
- Use language to your advantage.

Knowing **when** to contribute can be critical for communicating ideas. For instance, in a workshop setting, much of the first part of the day is usually spent getting "everyone on the same page". This may not be the best time to communicate your big idea. You may have better receptiveness if you save it until later. Likewise, communicating your idea during the closing moments of a meeting may be disastrous. By this time, the views of the attendees are already likely to be set and they will be focusing on their next task.

Knowing **how** to communicate is about you using a medium that your audience will prefer. You may have written a wonderful set of thoughts in a document, but this may not be the right route if your audience prefers face-to-face meetings. Be prepared to convert your message into different forms in order to appeal to your audience. Email, text messaging, voicemail, presentations, meetings, evening drinks, afternoon coffee, breakfast chats—anything at all will work, if it is in their preferred style.

Where to communicate may not always be a choice that is yours to make. Does your audience like a formal setting? A boardroom? Would they prefer something more casual? Don't let an inappropriate setting spoil things for others as in the example below.

The vicar loves the thrill of riding a motorcycle. We spoke while the parishioners were filing out of the church, twisting imaginary throttles with our wrists. Some of them had a quiet giggle at the two of us as they passed. Perhaps we chose the wrong place for this chat?

Regardless of what you know about your audience, if you cannot deliver your message with **clarity**, your idea will not be received. Sharing your idea only once may not be good enough either. Repeating it—perhaps in different styles or via different routes—is often necessary. There is a popular adage used for delivering speeches: "Tell them what you are going to say. Tell them. Then tell them what you said." This three-step process, or one like it, ensures that your message is clearly presented and that it has a good chance (three chances, in fact) of being received. Message clarity is also about appreciating nuances of language in different circumstances. Sensitivity—particularly across cultures—is always advisable. Consider the following.

> If you cannot deliver your message with clarity, your idea will not be received.

The bride's British mother sent a message to the groom's American family about the upcoming London wedding. She advised them not to worry about travel arrangements, between the ceremony and the reception, because she would be "laying on a bus". To the UK guests, this made perfect sense. However, the groom was left to explain to the Americans that his mother-in-law was not going to be lying prostrate on top of a bus.

Observing the body **language** of your audience is a good measure of your transmission and of their reception. Do they agree with you? Are they waiting to add to your thoughts? These are questions that can be partially answered by reading body language. For example, crossed arms is a good clue that you are not being heard. Boredom is classically shown when people look at their watch or fingernails. Someone who is on the same wavelength as you will tend to mimic your movements. You can rely on these and other body language signals from your audience.

Nigel Risner[1] suggests a lighthearted, zookeeper philosophy of communication, where personalities fall under one of four animal headings—monkeys, elephants, lions and dolphins. Each animal represents a set of characteristics and has its own linguistic preferences.

Monkeys, he says, are playful people and not very well focused. To communicate effectively with monkeys, they need a regular reminder that you are paying attention to them. Dolphins are selfless people. They are happiest when everyone else is happy. Lions see themselves as leaders and assume themselves to be right until proven wrong. Lions need to feel that your views are in line with theirs. Elephants endlessly process information and are slow to reach decisions. If you want to communicate effectively with an elephant, make sure that you provide lots of background information and that you put forward a watertight case. The beauty of this system is its simplicity and ease of application. You can design your own approach too. Remember to make it simple, memorable and enjoyable enough for you to apply it regularly.

Communicating your ideas well is a necessary step towards unleashing their full potential. Develop your idea. Get your story straight. Then share it in a way that enables others to keep it alive.

TRUTH

12

Half-thoughts need to be heard

A lot of your time is spent forming and sharing complete thoughts. Write a report. Build a presentation. Provide an agenda. In reality, you also share a large amount of incomplete thoughts, or half-thoughts, too. Everyone does. What we are not always so good at, however, is capturing half-thoughts and appreciating their creative value.

Half-thoughts are concepts, based on instinct, that will not necessarily have a completely determined direction. A half-thought is the foremost concept that you can recall when you unexpectedly talk through a topic with someone. It is not a prepared, calculated statement. Half-thoughts can appear in a sporadic fashion and at any time. When you swap them with a colleague, the outcome is an unplanned, organic conversation. Most half-thought conversations occur away from your desk, away from your reference points and when you are wholly dependent on what you choose to recall.

Half-thoughts can appear in a sporadic fashion and at any time.

Consider the following. You turn the corner in the corridor and find yourself face to face with a colleague. She slows for a moment and asks for your opinion about an upcoming event. You are away from your desk, your notes and your beloved computer. What do you do? Share a half-thought—an instinctive response based on the dominant thought that has stuck in your mind.

These informal moments can produce a good number of creative, engaging discussions and powerful insights. So, why is it that they are so undervalued, particularly by organisations?

Organisations are geared towards capturing and using complete thoughts only. They build systems and structures that ask for fully formed solutions. This is not just limited to reports, meetings, agendas and presentations. The need for complete thoughts begins with an unspoken, generally accepted point of view that the boss knows best. Only complete thoughts can be sent upwards through each level in the chain of command. In the end, this can lead to a sterile perspective landing on the decision-maker's desk. The exuberance of the initial concept is buried under pages of minutiae, risk mitigation and justifications.

Some organisations are worse because they penalise individuals for sharing a less than complete thought. Here, the insights of a half-thought can be ignored because an in-depth report has not been built. This can be soul destroying for the person sharing the thought, and they may not have the will afterwards to build a complete report. The result is that the thought—rightly or wrongly—withers away. The rest of the organisation hears the tale and feels that it is not worth bothering to present ideas to management, because the ideas will not be heard. Konosuke Matsushita,[1] the founder of Panasonic and a leading twentieth-century industrialist, once clearly illustrated this as a difference between Western and Eastern working philosophies:

> *We are going to win and the industrialised west is going to lose out. There is nothing you can do about it because the reasons for your failure are within yourselves. With your bosses doing the thinking, while the workers wield the screwdrivers, you are convinced deep down that this is the right way to do business. For you, the essence of management is getting ideas out of the heads of bosses into the hands of labour . . . For us, the core of management is the art of mobilising and putting together the intellectual resources of all employees in the service of the firm.[2]*

What half-thoughts can do for you

Matsushita's statement is stark but illuminating. Harnessing and empowering all the intelligence of a workforce is surely better than relying on just the few who happen to hold the most senior positions. A healthy half-thought culture is one where staff feel comfortable to submit ideas and where managers are genuinely eager to hear them. Rewarding and using half-thoughts, across all levels of the organisation, is part of improving organisational intelligence.

There are other benefits to valuing half-thoughts as well. They can help you to improve communications and to get your organisation talking about items of real concern. Half-thoughts are viral—they are not constrained by a chain of command. This trait helps an idea to speak for itself and to spread extensively. Communications remains one of the most common areas of focus when organisations try to improve. Most organisations would pounce at the chance to improve its ability to communicate.

Sharing half-thoughts is also a visible way to build and maintain relationships. The maintenance of healthy relationships within (and outside) an organisation is a key enabler of success. Ronald Coase described the power of relationships as the basic essence of a firm in his seminal work, *The Nature of the Firm* in 1937:

> *A firm, therefore, consists of the system of relationships which comes into existence when the direction of resources is dependent on an entrepreneur.*[3]

Half-thoughts assist relationship-building because they occur naturally and can be a preferred medium for many people. This is great for encouraging creative characteristics and can potentially be linked to the overall success of an organisation.

Half-thoughts have speed. They move round an organisation more quickly than complete thoughts. This means that they can have a positive impact on response times, adaptability and anticipatory thinking. Finally, valuing the use of half-thoughts can lead to a more satisfied workforce, one that feels it is being listened to and is involved in the decision-making process.

Half-thoughts are an important part of any successful creative formula. Truth 20 is about the specific ways that a team can harness and use half-thoughts.

Meanwhile, next time you bump into a colleague in the corridor, pause for a moment to ask for their opinion. Gather their thoughts about that nagging issue where you need to find a creative solution. It might prove to be one of the most valuable interruptions to your day.

13

Compare to create—the power of using metaphors

Metaphors are useful when expanding a thread of thought, or in communicating the essence behind an idea. A good metaphor tells a story that is related to the issue at hand, is easy to use and is quickly understood by all. Most importantly, metaphors are powerful in terms of highlighting a desired meaning.

A metaphor compares unlike things and, at the same time, sheds light on their common characteristics. When you compare the essence of two seemingly unrelated things, new linkages are formed. Also, you share deeper meaning and you see things anew. Metaphors are a potent way to guide others in new directions while still aiming towards the crux of an idea that you want to share. As an example, look below at a passage from W.H. Auden's *Funeral Blues*:

> When you compare the essence of two seemingly unrelated things, new linkages are formed.

He was my North, my South, my East and West,

My working week and my Sunday rest,

My noon, my midnight, my talk, my song;

I thought that love would last for ever: I was wrong.

There is no doubting the deep adoration and love that the admirer is sharing over the death of his dear friend. The connections drawn are poetic, not literal. Logically, a compass and a person are not related but philosophically, they will be for ever connected by the power of such a well-placed metaphor.

A great example of a metaphor used in a business context is when Apple's CEO Steve Jobs made this reference to the Mac OS X Aqua user interface:

We made the buttons on the screen look so good you'll want to lick them.[1]

It was a unique and captivating concept that stirred up the technology industry. It was also entirely apt for the amount of change that Apple was bringing to the market at the time. The metaphor provided deeper meaning of the company's intent.

This philosophical connection is why metaphors can be so useful in communicating the thinking that underpins an idea. Below is a metaphor of a different type. It is from the hugely popular *Hitchhiker's Guide to the Galaxy*, by Douglas Adams:

The ships hung in the sky in much the same way that bricks don't.[2]

Not content with only drawing a comparison, Adams adds irony and humour to his meaning. Did the spaceships look awkward and brick-like in the sky? Or is it just a humorous play with words? Does it matter, or is it enough that the image causes you to see things differently? These examples by Auden, Jobs and Adams illustrate the surprise connections and fresh perspective that a metaphor can produce.

The creative characteristics that metaphors can help you realise are as follows.

- **Powerful explanation**—They help to communicate the true meaning of ideas and introduce new thought directions to investigate.

- **Creative linkages**—Seeing the relationship of what was previously, unrelated.

- **Broader perspective**—This reveals new and interesting opportunities to consider.

- **Unblocks thinking**—This encourages you when thoughts are slowing down.

- **Invites freedom**—A good metaphor can serve as an invitation for others to be more abstract and open-minded in their thinking.

- **Surprise discovery**—When two unlike things are first compared, a moment of surprise happens, taking you into uncharted territory and away from the limits of in the box thinking.

So far, we have been discussing metaphors in a literary sense. This is their formal home and how they are usually encountered. You can use metaphors to your creative advantage when you write, like in the examples above. You can also use them when you speak, such as in a workshop setting or when you share stories. There are more avenues that you can use to create and express metaphors too. Drawing, modelling and other media styles, like music and film, are all excellent media that are available.

Drawing—even if at a stick figure level—can introduce a wealth of possibilities. Not only do you gain a comparison, but you see an image too. You can also get an indication of the size of the issues. If a team member draws your company as a ship and a current company issue as its anchor, that signifies one message. If the anchor is drawn at three times the size of the ship, that says something else entirely. Drawing can highlight both explicit and implied meaning. The relative size of the anchor to the ship, for instance, may only be a subconscious feature by the illustrator. Sometimes, completely accidental interpretations of drawings can be helpful too—"Well, it's meant to be a horse at the winning post, but I suppose it could be a frightened kitten running away."

Modelling introduces three-dimensional stories because of the physical shape and location of each model component. When modelling, it becomes easier to see relationships and issues. Questions come to life when working in three dimensions that might otherwise go unaddressed when using two dimensions. Why have you made him bigger? Is his role more important? Does he do the work of two people?

Other media forms, such as **film** or **music**, are enormously rich ways to communicate. You can use these methods to extend the metaphor into complete stories. Imagine if your team showed you a homemade film where they were employees stuck in the hopeless horror of the aftermath of a major catastrophe. Vermin. Disease. No rest. No resources. No information. No vision of an outcome. It would communicate a strong message to you, wouldn't it?

There are three ways that you can encourage the use of metaphors.

1. Explain to others the power of metaphors as a means of reaching greater understanding and conveying key thoughts. Demonstrate through your own examples where you can. Even one metaphor can drive your message home if it helps to explain an important issue.

> Even one metaphor can drive your message home if it helps to explain an important issue.

2. Give time to conversations that make comparisons or that ask people to describe what they mean in other words. These can be formal meetings or playful chats—either way they are the basis for building metaphors.

3. Build support for storytelling as a medium. Storytelling will naturally include metaphors, implied or explicit.

Metaphors are powerful instruments for helping you to see things in a new light. They have real explanative power when you need to convey a core meaning.

TRUTH

14

See what you see, not what
you think you ought to see

Try this quick exercise. Look at the sentence below and count the number of Fs.

FINISHED FILES ARE THE RESULT OF MANY YEARS OF SCIENTIFIC STUDY COMBINED WITH THE EXPERIENCE OF MANY YEARS.

How many do you see?[1]

Seeing what is actually in front of you is not always as clear-cut as it seems. Sometimes, you only see things that you *think* you ought to see. From a creative perspective, this can cause a number of problems.

- Key attributes of everyday items become temporarily "invisible" to you.

- You could miss out on important details.

- You develop blind spots—areas where you lack knowledge or experience, making it difficult to see things completely.

- You could temporarily lose interest in the topic.

All of this is possible, even when looking at a simple sentence, with a simple instruction, like the example above. Each time you see something other than what is in front of you, you run the risk of endangering your creative efforts. Let's look in more detail at the four circumstances listed above and how you can tackle them.

Failing to spot key attributes of **everyday items** is understandable. It happens to everybody as they hustle through busy lives and are exposed to a lot of information. However, if you give everyday topics a bit more of your attention, you might pick up on some high-quality insights.

Consider this example. Two friends were talking about the difficulties of adjusting from right-hand drive to left-hand drive cars, and vice versa. It is a common occurrence for people travelling between the UK and Europe, or between the UK and the USA. The first said that he had no problems with driving, until he came across an empty road with no other traffic. In these situations, he would momentarily freeze because he was unsure about which side of the road the car should be on. The second paused and said, "Just keep the steering wheel in the centre of the road, then you will always be on the correct side of the road."

When you assess everyday items more closely, you might find some common rules. When you think about why the everyday things around you exist the way they do, you could gain some lasting insights—like in the driving example above. Together, common rules and lasting insights help you to make more space for creative thinking.

> Together, common rules and lasting insights help you to make more space for creative thinking.

Missing the detail of a situation could mean that while you have a general appreciation of a matter, you could be overlooking important fundamentals, or straying too far away from the core issue. Be sure that you understand all aspects of the problem you face, before you set out to face it. Getting to grips with detail helps you to put your ideas on a solid footing. With a robust base in situ, you can creatively investigate other avenues with no worry. You can also refer back to your detailed understanding, in order to align your thoughts. Ultimately, paying heed to the detail will guarantee that your creative solution is in line with the original requirements.

Blind spots are bigger and uglier still. They occur when you lack information about a topic. Blind spots can turn up when you least expect them or develop over time. If you are aware that your blind spot exists, you can easily tackle the problem. You just seek out the help you need and the problem gets solved. A blind spot that develops over time is trickier to deal with. It develops because you get used to routine. You become set in your thinking. In many cases, you may not be aware that the blind spot has developed.

For example, one summer, a practice beach landing by the army interrupted my family holiday. The beach was closed for the day, but we were welcome to watch proceedings from the nearby cliff top. There were many vehicles—ships, landing craft, helicopters, troops and tracked equipment. While watching, I was amazed to see that little had changed with this process for several decades. It looked out of date. It also seemed to be completely out of step with the current asymmetric format of conflict used by terrorists and pirates. The entire exercise looked like a blind spot that was overdue to be found out.

Try to avoid blind spots by changing your routine. Alter the thinking patterns that you use. Vary, too, the people that you discuss ideas with. Consider checking your insights

Try to avoid blind spots by changing your routine.

with someone who sees the world differently from you. It might be a little uncomfortable at the time, but it will be much less painful than exposing your blind spot to everyone.

A loss of interest in a topic can be a problem, but only if you are unable to apply a creative approach, or if you have no one to turn to for help. If you are lumbered with looking at the same issue for the thousandth time, it makes sense that your interest might drop. To see the problem clearly, try to look at it from a wholly new perspective.

■ Look for the root cause (Truth 19).

■ Consider a new starting point (Truth 23).

■ Try a new information source (Truth 32).

In parallel to using a new approach, you can ask for help from someone who is more eager about the topic than you are. Not only will this help you to solve the problem that you face, but you might also get re-energised by the topic. You might also enjoy the solution that you build together.

Applying these guidelines will help you to limit the occasions when you only see what you think you ought to see. It will help you to focus on precisely what is in front of you with clarity, completeness and consistency.

TRUTH

15

Failure is good for you

Ask some friends for their greatest learning experiences and you are likely to hear about a failure or two. Failure is a great way to learn. Failure does not teach you more—or less—than success. It just teaches you different things. With success, you learn about how to be successful. With failure, you learn that you still need to learn. Success stories already steal too many headlines. Success gets the lion's share of our attention. For creative balance, you need to learn from both success and failure.

A note of clarity. This truth is written with a failed project or business in mind. Advocating failure is not the focus of this truth. Likewise, this truth does not suggest that if a project or business of yours fails, you become a failure. Everybody fails sometime. It is inevitable. This truth focuses on what you can learn from failure, when it happens.

The creative benefits that failure can provide, if you are prepared to learn, are many. Once you experience and emerge from a failed situation, you have access to unique knowledge. You will have faced dilemmas that required your considered decisions. You will have

The creative benefits that failure can provide, if you are prepared to learn, are many.

dealt with adverse changes to any plans laid. Maybe most importantly, you emerge knowing more about yourself. Each of these lessons can be useful in developing your creative characteristics. The following is a list of specific benefits you can take away from failure.

1. **On-the-job learning**—This learning happens in real time with real resources and gives you the chance to test your new knowledge in a live setting afterwards.

2. **Realism**—Failure provides lessons, sometimes hard ones. A dose of realism from a failure helps to churn out creative ideas that are also fully actionable.

3. **Identifying weaknesses**—With success you can only estimate your weaknesses; with failure you will get to know them very well. Knowing where you are weak is as important as knowing your strengths, in order to be your best creative self.

4. **Routes for success**—Failure in one area can shed light on opportunities for success in other directions.

5. **Developing alternatives**—Failure demands reaction because your original plans will have gone awry. Failure causes you to think creatively about developing other options.

6. **Dealing with stress**—The process of failing is different from success. Decisions can get hair-raising. You are faced with limited choices, sometimes with harsh outcomes. Behaviours become critical. As a result, you learn about the skills and support that you rely on in stressful situations. You also learn how to leverage these.

7. **Character forming**—You find a level of personal resolve that is difficult to attain by any other means.

8. **Overcoming fear**—Fear of failure can be debilitating for many people. It can prevent risk-taking and encourage a culture that lacks confidence. However, emerging from a failed activity can break down this fear, giving you renewed confidence.

9. **Preparation**—By experiencing failure, you mentally construct a preventative checklist for the future. You have a clearer idea about warning signs and you know the response to use if failure knocks again.

Experiencing failure also indicates some positive things about you. It says that you have been through a complete life cycle process—start, growth (or not), maturity, realisation of the inevitable and finish.

> Experiencing failure indicates some positive things about you.

Emerging as a survivor of a failure gives you a rare chance to focus on the most critical aspects of your personal make-up. You locate your inner strength. You find values that you depend on and a clarity of perspective that you may not have had before.

In some cultures, like the USA, failure is generally seen as absolutely necessary and can even be worn as a badge of respect. "I've failed and lived to tell the tale." Some brilliant, and highly creative, people openly share their stories of failure in very public ways.

- J.K. Rowling, creator of Harry Potter, delivered the 2008 Harvard University commencement speech, focusing on failure and imagination.[1]

- James Dyson, the prolific inventor, maintains a web presence that tells his story (including 5,127 prototypes made over a five-year period).[2]

- Steve Jobs, CEO of Apple, delivered the 2005 Stanford University commencement speech. He concentrates on three personal stories, all touching on failure.[3]

Having a handful of high-profile stories is comforting when you look for the positives of failure. There is more that you can do too.

First, you should get an understanding of why the failure happened. Was it out of your control, as in a broad market failure? Or was it within your control and developed due to your own execution issues? Was it a mixture of both? Review the steps that led to the failure. Is there any way that failure could have been detected earlier or even avoided completely? Have you put systems in place to prevent further failure? Reasons for failure can be varied—poor judgement, lack of experience, wrong decisions, unexplored options, inadequate preparation, unachievable vision, missing strategy, lack of motivation, absence of financial muscle and bad timing are a few common ones. Failing systems consume creative time and space. Removing them will give you future creative manoeuvrability.

Second, you should review the expectations held at the outset of the task. Were these realistic? Were the objectives clear and attainable? Were the original plan and expectations aligned from the start?

Third, you must separate the act of failing from thinking of yourself as a failure. Everybody fails. It happens every day. It is inevitable. Do not focus on the fact that failure has occurred, focus instead on what you can learn from it. Take the positives from failure and use them to attain future success.

> Take the positives from failure and use them to attain future success.

Failure is not what you set out to achieve, granted. Yet, it never occurs without the reward of having learned something from it. In fact, there are only two circumstances where failure has no positives to bring. First, when it is ignored and not recognised as having happened. Second, when we elect not to learn from failure. Which begs the question—with so much learning on offer, why would you ever choose to ignore the lessons of failure?

TRUTH

16

Brainstorming is not the only technique

Brainstorming is the creative technique that you are probably most familiar with. It is well known and widely used. Businesses use it to develop products and services. Writers apply it to overcome temporary mental blocks. Trainers use it to assist team-building exercises. It is a first port of call for just about anyone who is looking to develop a host of new ideas. Brainstorming, however, is not the only creative tool at your disposal.

Backgrounder on brainstorming

Brainstorming is a group discussion that encourages the members to generate new ideas about an issue. It also postpones the analysis of ideas until later in the process. Brainstorming has existed casually for some time, but it was Alex Osborn, a founder of the advertising agency BBDO, who formally introduced it in 1948 with his book, *Your Creative Power*. Four basic rules were established then, which are as follows.

- Generate as many ideas as possible.
- Do not criticise.
- No idea is too wacky or unusual.
- Try to combine ideas.

Brainstorming sessions can be a great way to bring a team together and to access their knowledge. Brainstorming can also be a way to expand a specific topic in quick time. As a tool, it is easy to understand and apply. It is the longstanding workhorse of creative thinking.

Techniques beyond brainstorming

In the creative area, diversity exists in the number of tools available, how you can use them and what they can help you to accomplish. The three techniques in the following story may not be the first alternatives to brainstorming that pop into your mind, but they do introduce the concept of varying your approach.

Diversity exists in the number of tools available, how you can use them and what they can help you to accomplish.

Once I was aboard a ship for three days with a few hundred advertising agency employees. These guys were brainstorming zealots. As a guest speaker, I was virtually the only potential client, among dozens of agencies, on the vessel. Eager salesmen tracked me down at every turn. During a break, I threw a question to each of the agencies that approached me. I asked, "If brainstorming is a decades-old concept, what else do you do?" Most of them were flummoxed by the question and stumbled through their answers. One group responded immediately and confidently, though: "We do Shamanism, Paganism and Trance[1]—which would you like?"

Techniques beyond brainstorming can be grouped into two broad areas—namely:

- helping teams to generate a lot of ideas;
- putting creativity into action.

Tools from both areas are outlined below. Each tool has a truth dedicated to it elsewhere in this book, which expands the topic in more detail.

Helping teams to generate a lot of ideas

The following eight tools are, like brainstorming, easily applied in teams of people. They are easy to understand and communicate. These are particularly good tools to use if you want to generate a lot of ideas.

1. **Using metaphors**—By attaching comparisons to seemingly unlike items, you can readily expand thoughts, establish new thought directions or share underlying meaning of a concept (see Truth 13).

2. **Find the root cause**—Look carefully at separating symptoms from causes, understanding dependencies and ensuring that your creative focus is applied effectively (see Truth 19).

3. **Start from a different place**—Avoid the pitfall of beginning an exciting, expansive, creative exploration in a routine, corporate, paralysing way (see Truth 23).

4. **Change your perspective**—This enables you to see something in one way and then to view it in a completely

different light, bringing new insights to the fore (see Truth 25).

5. **Empathy**—It is not always the case that needs can be articulated. Sometimes, you uncover them by being empathetic towards why people do the things they do (see Truth 26).

6. **Complete the pattern**—Study patterns around you, understand the systems they are part of and deconstruct these to uncover fundamental insights (see Truth 27).

7. **Try a new source**—Reading widely is the smart way to appreciate alternative viewpoints and to improve your creative skills (see Truth 32).

8. **New connections**—Stop talking to the same sets of people and start talking instead to some new groups, such as communities that are eager to share their ideas with you (see Truth 36).

Putting creativity into action

Any idea generated is really only as good as the solution that eventually gets put in place. Turning your good ideas into solutions requires tools that hone the initial idea and furthers its development. Each of the tools below provides a greater emphasis on implementation and execution.

1. **A £10 creativity budget**—You needn't spend a fortune on your creative activities. In fact, keeping a low profile can have its benefits too (see Truth 24).

2. **Build momentum**—Buy-in is a pipe dream; what you really need for ideas to succeed is organisational momentum (see Truth 33).

3. **Seed ideas in a hothouse**—Protect and nurture new ideas to help get them off to a solid start (see Truth 41).

4. **Dare to share**—Keeping your ideas isolated under a bushel is no good. Instead, dare to integrate your work, involve others and communicate success (see Truth 42).

5. **Quality, acceptance and execution**—This is the formula for creating lasting, truly valuable ideas (see Truth 43).

One last tool

There is one more tool available to you that Alex Osborn did not have: the internet. It has huge implications for your ability to explore a wealth of information and to share ideas with a global audience, at the touch of a button. It is taken for granted, but the internet remains a key creative device.

The internet remains a key creative device.

Brainstorming is a wonderful creative tool. However, a variety of other tools can also lead you to different insights and will enable you to appeal to a wider set of personalities. Having a number of creative approaches will keep your thinking fresh and provide added stimulus.

17

Test the validity of ideas with a five-minute business plan

If you are going to make your ideas come to fruition, you need to test their validity. Building a five-minute business plan is a great way to do this. You can see whether your ideas are on-topic, achievable and robust. A five-minute plan allows you to think through the detail of putting your ideas into action. It also gives you answers to questions that will arise when you start to share your idea with others.

Your five-minute business plan needs to address key questions about aims, market conditions, resources, risks and so on. By breaking your planning into stages, you can expertly tackle the following key areas.

1. Generate ideas.
2. Evaluate and take the best ideas forward.
3. Describe the best ideas in more detail.
4. Identify the key steps.
5. Capture the information.
6. Compare your surviving ideas.
7. Choose the winning idea(s).

1. Generate ideas

This is actually a pre-planning activity. Start by building ideas on the topic. Use a range of techniques, as needed. When you have considered the topic from several perspectives and amassed a number of ideas, you are ready to evaluate.

What it might look like: Dozens of ideas written on sticky notes, flip charts or paper.

2. Evaluate and take the best ideas forward

Evaluate and filter to select the best ideas and to eliminate weaker ones. Measure your ideas against key criteria in a matrix. Typical criteria could be time, feasibility, associated risk, idea fit (with the organisational ethos, values or brand), impact and

Evaluate and filter to select the best ideas and to eliminate weaker ones.

return on investment. Then, rate the suitability of your ideas against each of the key criteria—a number scale or ticks and crosses will do.

Another method is to compare two criteria at a time, expressed in terms of *low* and *high*. Make a simple graph with an x and y axis. For example, you might plot *impact* (what the idea will accomplish) against *time* (how long it will take to have the desired impact). Rate your ideas by plotting each on the graph. Ideas that are low in both aspects should be dropped. Ideas that are high in both can go forward. A decision will need to be taken about the ideas that lie in between.

What it might look like: If assessing on your own, you could draw a matrix on paper. If working with a team in a workshop, the matrix could be drawn on a flip chart and discussed. If you are working with others remotely, you could build a document and circulate it. Final selection might involve a team vote to limit the number of ideas that you take forward. Perhaps less than ten ideas will survive for the remaining stages.

3. Describe the best ideas in more detail

You will now have a small pool of higher potential ideas. Describe these in more detail. What does the existing market for each idea look like? Think about the resources that will be required—for example, people, time and money. Estimate these with quick calculations. State any assumptions behind your estimates. How much time will be needed to turn the ideas into reality? Think of the specific risks that could occur and what you would have to do to overcome these. Evaluate the risks on a simple scale of high, medium or low.

What it might look like: Build a generic format of questions that you see as most critical. Apply this format to each of the ideas. If in a workshop, separate into groups and work on different ideas. Groups should feed back the results of their discussions.

4. Identify the key steps

Now, order the detail from stage 3. Think about three things:

- Where are we now?
- Where do we want to go?
- How will we get there?

Describe the situation of where you are now in a quick summary. When thinking about where you want to go, describe what a successful outcome would look like. When thinking about how you will get there, cite how hurdles will be

Look for steps that appear to be particularly important and highlight them.

overcome. Look for steps that appear to be particularly important and highlight them. These might feel like critical junctures, or *turning points* that simply must happen if the idea is to be a success. For example: "Once we secure a sponsor we can really get moving."

What it might look like: Understand the order and relative importance of events by expressing them in a simple roadmap. Important steps will be highlighted.

5. Capture the information

Write down the results. This will help you to compare the ideas and could be useful when you address a similar topic in the future. You may be surprised later, when ideas are put into action, that your five-minute plan was pretty close to the actual solution.

What it might look like: A single sheet of paper describing the development of each idea.

6. Compare your surviving ideas

Return to your original evaluation matrix (**stage 2**). See whether you feel differently now about any of the marks given to some of the criteria. Think too about receptiveness to each idea. Will the idea generate enthusiastic support? You might be asked to help execute the chosen idea. If so, what essential outcomes do you expect?

What it might look like: Revisit the matrix. Review the idea summary statements. If working as a team, ask the team for a final vote and a short statement of supporting evidence.

7. Choose the winning idea(s)

By now, you will have enough information to select the ideas that you want to recommend. You will know what you like about them and why this is the case. You will be able to express the ideas as a complete story, from start to finish.

How many to select? One clear winner is always nice. However, it can help to present your recommendation alongside one or two second-best ideas, pointing out the key differences.

What it might look like: A summary presentation.

Learning how to evaluate your ideas gives you the means to put forward solid concepts with real potential. It could improve the number of your ideas that get implemented—and that go on to successful outcomes. Like Samuel Goldwyn once said, "The harder I work, the luckier I get."

TRUTH

18

An ounce of process delivers
pounds of success

See whether this sounds familiar. You sit down for a few minutes and complete some clues of a crossword puzzle (sudoku, if you prefer). After a period of concentration, your answers dry up and you leave the puzzle to press on with your daily chores. Hours later—maybe even at the end of the day—you pick up the crossword again. Almost immediately, your mind finds some solutions to clues that you did not have before. The odd thing is that you have not actively thought about the crossword all day long. So the question is, where did those new solutions come from? Why did leaving the puzzle alone deliver new answers when your earlier focus had exhausted your ideas?

The answer lies in appreciating how the mental process of creativity happens. Bringing together two things in a new and interesting way—making associations—is the heart of creativity. However, the process of making associations does not always thrive during focused, attentive thought periods. In fact, making creative associations might even be hampered by a steady period of focused concentration. Research suggests that conscious thought is the best environment for analytical processing and problem-solving.[1] In contrast, unconscious thought, or inattentiveness, is ideal for making creative associations.

> Unconscious thought, or inattentiveness, is ideal for making creative associations.

Inattentiveness also allows associations to be made over a broader base of information. In short, unconscious thought is great for solving complex problems. By not paying attention, by purposely diverting your attention away from a complex problem, you could be increasing your chances of creative thinking success.

Think of the crossword again. First, you focus on trying to solve as much as you can. Soon you reach your natural limit for conscious thinking. When you are away from the puzzle, you are unconsciously processing information. When you return, your mind has found new answers.

There are a couple of noteworthy corollaries to bear in mind, however. First, unconscious thought cannot create new knowledge, just new connections. You still need conscious thought to provide a base of information to be inattentive about. Second, unconscious thought only works better than conscious thought when there is a goal to focus on. Without a goal, inattention is not much more than aimless meandering.

What does this mean in terms of you applying a creative process? What should it look like? Wouldn't it be great if you could apply a process that delivered pounds of creative success?

Three things seem to be key. To begin with, your creative process should always have an aim in mind. In addition, both conscious and unconscious thinking should be allowed for. Finally, any unconscious time does not necessarily have to be quiet thinking time. It can be distractions—such as working on other issues. In fact, focusing on other issues will keep you from thinking about the original problem, while improving your efficiency, because you are thinking about more than one topic at a time.

Many years ago, I read a newspaper article discussing something that struck me as the ideal creative process. It seemed to account for both focused, concentrated thinking and unconscious, inattentive thinking. The article was called "Keep it simple", and the author discussed an obscure scientific theory called Jardin's Principle.[2]

Jardin: the meta-process for creativity

Jardin's Principle states that when trying to appreciate a system, your understanding passes through three levels. These levels are simplistic, complicated and then simple again. Complexity, it appears, is a natural step towards a more profound understanding. Complexity should not be managed, or avoided, as popular opinion suggests. Instead, complexity should be celebrated. This leads to a neater description of Jardin's three levels—simple, complex and profound.

> Complexity, it appears, is a natural step towards a more profound understanding.

Think of a toddler, pretending to drive by holding a rubber ring. He rotates the ring, makes a brrm, brrm noise and, as far as he is concerned, is driving. He is at a simple level of Jardin. Now consider a beginner driver. Her world is one of fretting over details like brakes, mirrors, traffic and other drivers. Add in environmental controls like the radio and air conditioning and you can see how she is at a complex level of Jardin. Finally, think about an experienced driver. He jumps in and drives off, almost without thinking about it. Mr Experience still performs a lot of complex driving tasks; he just has a profound understanding of driving now.

By mapping Jardin's levels against focused and inattentive thought, discussed earlier in this truth, you can see a pretty solid fit:

	Stage 1	Stage 2	Stage 3
Creative thinking	Focused thought	Inattentive thought	Focused thought
Jardin	Simple	Complex	Profound

- Stage 1—focus your thoughts to gain a simple understanding of the topic.
- Stage 2—add complexity by purposely introducing diversions.
- Stage 3—return to focused thought to reach a more profound understanding.

By recognising Jardin's Principle in your activities—by knowing that the passage through complexity is progress—you can build more, and better, creative solutions. Jardin's Principle bravely introduces complexity as necessary in order to reach a profound state, and it is in accord with research on focused and inattentive thought. It is an ideal description of the creative process at a high level.[3] The

> Complexity needs to happen in your creative activities.

important aspect for you to appreciate is that complexity needs to happen in your creative activities. It is OK to have a period where things start getting messy, because you know that they will emerge better as a result of the complexity. A quote, attributed to Oliver Wendell Holmes Jr, summarises the importance of the stages of Jardin:

I would not give a fig for the simplicity this side of complexity, but I would give my life for the simplicity on the other side of complexity.

Make sure that you purposely insert a diversion into the midst of your creative problem-solving. The diversion will ensure that everyone involved consciously leaves the problem alone while unconsciously continuing to address it. If you do not, you could miss out on a better, more profound answer.

TRUTH

19

Symptoms and causes first, ideas after

A farmer once told me this: "When a storm destroys your fence, you've got two problems. One is to mend the fence. The other is to catch the cows." This farmer's wisdom illustrates how a single cause can create more than one symptom. When your role is to find creative solutions, you will want to know whether you are addressing a symptom or an underlying cause. Symptoms are issues that are evident and obvious. *Catching loose cows and mending fence rails.* Causes are usually hidden and take a little more work to identify. *Why did the fence break and can it be prevented in future?*

The key to locating causes is to be aware of *context* when someone is sharing *content*. Here is an example. Ask a friend to tell you who their favourite film star is. You will most likely get two answers—their favourite star and why this is so. For example, "I like Morgan Freeman, particularly because of his role in The Shawshank Redemption." The star is the content, while the "why" portion of their answer is the context. Context is often given freely without you having to ask for it. You just need to look out for it.

When you do hear context being given, pursue it. In doing so, you will spend more time on a topic that holds substantial meaning for the other person, rather than chasing too many lesser issues. Or, as one Chinese proverb puts it, "If you chase two rabbits, both will escape."

> When you do hear context being given, pursue it.

Finding an underlying cause is helpful in developing ideas and making decisions about the future. When you are working creatively with a known cause, you gain some immediate benefits.

- You see the issue with more clarity.
- You make new connections.
- Relationships can emerge, such as commonality between symptoms or a cause that branches into more than one symptom.
- You will find underlying meaning that could redefine the issue.
- Key drivers are made evident.
- You will avoid drawing inaccurate assumptions.

At times, you will need to uncover context if it is not freely offered. To unearth an underlying cause, you will need a way to dig deeper—a way to analyse. Your approach should be adaptable, suitable for groups or for working alone and easy to convey to others. Five Whys is just such a method.

Five Whys

Asking "why" is a natural human condition that is a core component of your creative potential, as outlined in Truth 2. Young children remind us how to ask this question, just by frequent usage. With the passage of time, and the arrival of structured influences, this innate

> Asking "why" is a natural human condition that is a core component of your creative potential.

skill is subdued, however. Asking "why" is the cornerstone of philosophy too. It was Socrates who stated that "the only true wisdom is that you know nothing". His very manner of questioning, often of people's faith in popular opinions at the time, led to the foundations of Western philosophical dialogue. The technique of asking Five Whys is a solid way to revive and apply inquisitive examination.

It was the emergence of Japanese management processes in the 1950s and 1960s that brought the concept of Five Whys to the fore. Sakichi Toyoda, the founder of Toyota Industries, is said to have invented the concept. His model states that you should ask "why" five times in order to reach true understanding. In practice, the number can vary, but five iterations is judged to be a good amount.

It was while an employee of Toyota that Taiichi Ohno, the father of the widely studied Toyota Production System,[1] popularised Toyoda's Five Whys as a management tool. Ohno believed that you should "ask 'why' five times about every matter" in order to bring greater understanding. Mr Ohno often explained the approach of getting to the heart of a matter by telling a story of a welding machine robot that had broken down during a demonstration[2]:

1. Why did the robot stop?
The circuit has overloaded, causing a fuse to blow.

2. Why is the circuit overloaded?
There was insufficient lubrication on the bearings, so they locked up.

3. Why was there insufficient lubrication on the bearings?
The oil pump on the robot is not circulating sufficient oil.

4. Why is the pump not circulating sufficient oil?
The pump intake is clogged with metal shavings.

5. Why is the intake clogged with metal shavings?
Because there is no filter on the pump.

However, in your creative problem-solving, you may want to find alternative ways to ask "why". If you just repeat "why" in parrot fashion at your next team meeting, you might gain better problem understanding, but you could equally incense a few colleagues. Open-ended questions can help you, as they seek more than a one-word answer. They encourage a fuller response that involves feelings and personal insights. Below are some open-ended questions that are good alternatives to asking "why":

■ How did you respond?

■ What does that mean to you?

■ What kind of outcome were you expecting?

■ How did that make you feel?

■ How is that important to you?

■ What changes would you like to see?

■ What were you thinking about at the time?

■ How did that happen?

Five Whys is a great way to hear context and uncover causes. Asking "why", and "why" again, gives you the capacity to build lasting solutions. It will also help you to:

■ ensure that the problem is the right one to address and is fully defined;

■ identify relationships across symptoms and their causes;

■ find a single root cause, or the most important few causes, to concentrate on.

More than anything, applying Five Whys will enable you to know what you should—and should not—be addressing with your creative time. St Francis of Assisi said as much centuries ago:

Lord grant me the serenity to accept the things I cannot change, the courage to change the things I can, and the wisdom to know the difference.

When you can locate and work on causes rather than symptoms, you will be able to build a more systemic, creative solution to the issue you face. Look for context. Ask "why". Be selective about what you address.

TRUTH

20

You can teach your colleagues to use half-thoughts

Half-thoughts, as you saw in Truth 12, are instinctive, unprepared responses that will not have a completely defined direction. When you explore a half-thought with a colleague, the outcome is an unplanned, organic—*entirely creative*—conversation. A conversation where minds are racing to locate thoughts and to convey them accurately in quick time. Unfortunately, half-thoughts are often undervalued and are poorly used by organisations. In this truth, we will look at vehicles that you and your colleagues can creatively apply to make the best use of half-thoughts in your organisation.

Where you work

If your role requires you to be alone in an office quite a bit, or if you are someone who needs a lot of personal space and time at your desk, then you could be lacking access to half-thoughts. Mixing in with others is an obvious response, at least for part of your day. One of the best ways to do this is by using a shared workspace. Ideally, the table will be a single, flat surface, not a few desks pushed together. There will be no fixed seat locations and no partitions between people. A shared tabletop brings the following two half-thought sharing situations to the fore.

- You are exposed to more information and a regular diet of other people's thoughts and working styles.

- You are able to opt in or out of neighbouring conversations.

Casual sharing is the very basis of half-thoughts. You elect when to jump in and when to keep your distance. This self-selection of topics is something you already do in other environments, like at a drinks party.

> Casual sharing is the very basis of half-thoughts.

At a drinks party, you are engaged in your immediate conversation, but you are also aware of other happenings. Background conversations. Shifting chairs. Music. A familiar face in the crowd. You use your senses to drift in and out of your immediate conversation, while pursuing other thoughts. You end up focusing on the thoughts that interest you most—not all of them at once. The large number of stimuli do not cause mental overload, but they do lead you to choose where you pay attention. In a shared working space, this is still true. There are more stimuli, but you retain control and elect to get involved in the material of most interest to you. As a result, more information is shared, robust decision-making is in place, camaraderie develops and a positive feeling of liberation spreads through the team.

How you share

You can create conditions for sharing half-thoughts. For example, calling a meeting and giving only limited preparation time means that everyone will need to rely on their salient thoughts—not prepared feedback. Another way to capture half-thoughts at meetings is to include a few minutes of impromptu thinking time at an otherwise pre-planned meeting. The impromptu element could (maybe should) be entirely different from the main meeting topic. It can be broad discussions, comparison/contrasting viewpoints, list-building—just about anything that gets the team to think on the go and to share their thoughts. Before your next meeting, consider stirring up some half-thoughts by using some of the suggested impromptu topics below.

- What is your favourite product and why?
- What brands do you adore and why?
- If our organisation was in industry X, which company would we most look like?
- Describe your best holiday.
- Discuss any "top ten" list—greatest inventions, rock bands, leaders, etc.

Even with just a few minutes of free-thinking, you and your colleagues will share half-thoughts and give insights into your individual thinking styles. Both will help to stimulate new ideas in the team. Sometimes, this kind of conversation happens quite naturally before a meeting starts and no prompting is required. Next time you see it happening, do not rush to start the meeting. Remember that even in a lighthearted chat, half-thoughts are being shared and insights are developing in the team.

How you nurture

Half-thoughts can be nurtured in locations that stimulate a casual exchange of ideas. Seating spaces, community areas and vending locations are a few examples of physical zones. Here, conversations can easily veer away from current work-in-progress. They are natural half-thought generators. Disappointingly, they can suppress half-thoughts if the spaces themselves are uninspiring.

Nurturing half-thoughts can also come from some seemingly incidental office items. Having the best coffee on the floor, a supply of tasty treats or even a good knowledge of the local area are just three examples. Each of these examples invites people into your space, under a casual banner and could lead to interesting exchanges.

How you capture

The capture of half-thoughts is vital if you are to get best use of them. Formal innovation programmes are a good start. Employees are encouraged to submit their ideas to a clearing house, which investigates them and allocates the idea within the organisation. These programmes need complementary reward and communication programmes to encourage regular participation.

> The capture of half-thoughts is vital if you are to get best use of them.

Separately, it is important to encourage individuals to keep track of the most exciting insights that they have themselves or have witnessed. Personal notebooks are the simplest way. In addition, you might consider a regular review session of half-thoughts that have been uncovered. A more visual and interactive approach is to build an ideas wall—a place to post the most exciting half-thoughts that people find. An ideas wall, which is regularly updated, can be very useful as a discussion guide and an attractor for still more thoughts.

By considering where you work, how you share and how you nurture half-thoughts, you will increase your exposure to them. In these exchanges, you are never completely sure of whom you might meet and what you might discuss. The conversations will always be spontaneous and explorative. After a bit of practice of capturing half-thoughts, you will soon assemble a mosaic of insights regarding your organisation. The product is a creative dream—an engine room that inspires thoughts and a means to fast track those thoughts into your organisation.

TRUTH

21

Newsflash—insanity and routine are not worlds apart

It was Albert Einstein who said this about routine: "Insanity: doing the same thing over and over again and expecting different results." His message is clear— if you want new results, you must do new things. Doing something novel is at the core of creativity. There are times, however, when trying to suggest new approaches is likely to fall on deaf ears. Creative blockages require creative solutions. Below are four common log-jam situations with explanation on how you can overcome them.

Log-jam 1—"We just don't get on with those guys"

Not getting on with someone can be completely debilitating. This is true for individuals and for teams of people. It can put an end to any creative effort you start. Having an honest, heart-to-heart chat is still the most reliable way to iron out differences. But when the relationship needs ongoing attention, you could apply a little creativity to the way that you engage.

A new setting may be all that you need. Have you considered holding conversations while picnicking or walking in the park? For longstanding relationship issues, however, you might need more than a new venue.

For example, Orange, like many other companies, had a longstanding difference of perspective between Engineering and Marketing. The product, a mobile phone, is technical, but it was marketed as a lifestyle choice. This regularly put the Pointy Heads (Engineering) and Fluffy Heads (Marketing) at odds with each other. Trust was not always evident. Growing tired of this, the Pointy Heads invented a forum called Doohickey Day.[1] Here, they invited the Fluffy Heads and shared knowledge with them. Technical language and engineering jargon were banned. In fact, they made it fun for the Fluffy Heads by allowing them to "buzz in" if any presenter used jargon. At the end of the day, the Pointy Head who had received the most buzzes received a penance—he had to go to work for a day with the Fluffy Heads. The result was a fun and fact-filled day that brought the two disparate groups together each year.

Log-jam 2—"I don't know where to look"

It was not so long ago that people had access to only a few television channels, a handful of radio stations and absolutely no web pages. In those days, Walter Cronkite, a widely respected US news anchor, used to end his evening broadcasts with the phrase, "And that's the way it is." With so few other choices, you could turn the TV off and feel that Walter was right—*that's the way it is*. These days, your choices for information are virtually unlimited. In addition to more sources of radio and television, you have immense access to relatively new tools like referrals, trust webs and interest groups—for example, Amazon, epinions.com and 43things.com.[2]

Before a telephone interview with a writer, I asked a researcher to locate some background information on the caller. After the call, I asked the researcher how he was able to find such detailed information so quickly. He sheepishly admitted that he had used the author description off Amazon. Even though he had done no research, the information was still useful to me and, importantly, just as trusted.

Do not be afraid to look right under your nose, either. Solutions to work issues can be found at work, but they can also be found at home. Sometimes obviously. Be open to solutions that arrive from other areas of your life.

> Be open to solutions that arrive from other areas of your life.

Log-jam 3—"The boss kills all of my ideas"

Rejection of foreign ideas does unfortunately happen sometimes. Here is a simple three-step way to get a "prickly boss to eat out of your creative paw paw".

- Ask the boss for their top ten issues.
- Find their preferred way to receive information.
- Get busy delivering what *you* think is required, in the order *they* need it and in the way *they* want it.

"Bring me solutions not problems" was a mantra of a former prickly boss. I soon learned to bring ideas to him presented with three options. One would be my preferred solution, the other two were runners-up. By doing this, we were soon on the same wavelength and sharing successful ideas, solutions and progress.

Log-jam 4—"That idea will never work"

It is always frustrating to hear someone trying to stop an idea before it can be heard properly. Frequently, the person killing the idea is doing so because they are second-guessing what their managers will want. This filtration of ideas means that decision-makers are sometimes fed on a regular diet of similar information, with few new ideas getting through successfully.

Getting your idea beyond these filters requires some bold creativity. One solution is to place your idea within a rumour and start sharing it. Rumour bypasses the idea filters and puts the concept in the hands of others. Rumour usually travels faster than company reports, especially if it is juicy, so you will have early feedback too. Soon, the rumour will live—or die—of its own accord. If it lives, so does your idea.

> Rumour bypasses the idea filters and puts the concept in the hands of others.

Consider this story. A friend's concept for an advertising campaign looked to be solid. The problem was that no one along the management route had any interest in it. Dismayed, he turned to what he felt was his last resort—he made it up! He made mock-up advertisements of the new campaign. Then, in quiet periods, he replaced existing images along the corridors with his made-up adverts. They were in keeping with the style of other campaigns and did not look out of place. Soon, discussions started about the posters. They were quickly verified as unofficial by the marketing department, but not before management considered the campaign as a viable solution. His suggestion was not ultimately taken on board, but he was absolutely successful in getting it beyond the idea filters and into the boardroom.

Creativity asks you to consider new routes in order to reach new solutions. Trying to approach things from different points of view, or to persist with an idea, is not insane. It is what is required. It is just what Einstein might have done, so you are in good company.

TRUTH

22

Set your limits on limitless thinking

Creativity is not a free-for-all, limitless thinking festival—although this view persists in some places. Boundaries are needed for creativity, just as they are needed elsewhere. Boundaries give focus and direction. Creative boundaries are needed less for fencing you in and more for identifying what is off-limits. This way, they do not interfere with the creative process and they keep idea generation focused on the end goal. By putting boundaries in place, you employ the best of left-brain, creative thinking and right-brain, logical frameworks.

To set some limits on limitless thinking, you should take the following three steps.

1. Frame the topic.
2. Name the type of challenge.
3. Involve the people and resources you need.

Step 1—Frame the topic

Framing the topic is the easiest step. State what is in and out of your investigation. For example, "What we are focusing on is the station experience; not train travel itself." A simple phrase can help to summarise the position. The key is to express precisely what you mean by the topic. Give some solid definition. For example, "In what way will the function of cities change ten years in the future?" Avoid generalities. Once a specific frame is in place, you might share a few subsets that you intend to investigate. For example, "We'll look at the role of government, technological developments and society's response."

> State what is in and out of your investigation.

Step 2—Name the type of challenge

The challenge type is the overall method that you plan to use to address the issue. Are you conducting research? Do you hope to influence someone or a group? Will you use a competition to encourage participation? Each is a viable option. How you choose to investigate is up to you. It is dependent on the type of outcome that you want to achieve and the resources that you have available. Below are a few ways to set out your creative challenge.

- **Research**—A great approach if you are looking to lay creative groundwork in a new area.

- **Thought leadership**—A new or original idea is valuable as a way to set out new directions. It can provide an organisation with a new strategic position, setting it apart from its competition. New ideas can also deliver the advantage of competitive lead times when developing new goods and services.

- **Competition**—A competition can be very good for seeking input from a large population. It can also encourage participation over a sustained period. Think in advance about how you want to measure the submitted ideas. These could be cost to implement, time required, resources needed, wackiness of the concept, idea quality and so on.

- **Quest**—You may have a clear vision in mind or a goal that has been passed on to you from the organisation. Use this end goal with those who are helping you to think through the concept. Keep the discussions and explorations focused on the end goal. The whole process will be creative but also more solution-oriented.

In all cases, try to make your challenge type clear and engaging. It needs to focus the minds of the people involved and to draw out creative ideas.

Try to make your challenge type clear and engaging.

Step 3—Involve the people and resources you need

Who to involve in your creative exercise is up to you. A lot will depend on the tone that you hope to achieve. Do you need to base your eventual solution on expert opinions? How will you ensure that you get some fresh perspectives? Do you want to stir up current thinking? Once you know the tone of your exploration, invite people with a diverse set of perspectives to participate. Diversity will ensure that you get new ideas, challenge conventional thinking and draw out a healthy debate among the participants.

To maintain energy levels you may need to vary the way that you engage. On a day-to-day basis, manage the energy levels by knowing when to stop. Most people cannot be creative all day. Chat in advance about the preferred creative thinking time for everyone. Below are a few specific ways to vary your approach occasionally and to keep a high level of engagement.

- **Think tank**—This format involves lots of discussion, whether free-ranging or focused.

- **Desk-based**—Working individually at desks may not sound creative, but it can be. Set and share expectations with each person. Make sure that everyone knows their topic to investigate and the topics of their colleagues. This will help the group to act as one team, depending on each other for specific input. Then send them back to investigate. Get the group to share information regularly. This will make progress visible and keep interest levels high.

- **Away days**—Getting the group out to a different location can be an inspired move on your part. Select a location that is unlike your normal environment. Just another boring, windowless hotel conference room is unlikely to provide people with the kind of inquisitiveness that you want them to apply.

- **Treasure hunts**—Go out with colleagues to find examples of aspects of the topic being discussed. For the train station example used earlier, a treasure hunt might involve "discovering" great entrances, the best fast food, the most popular public furniture, and so on.

In addition to the three steps above, you will need to consider the time you will apply to the creative exercise. It is no good taking six months to develop a perfect solution when an answer is required in six weeks—or six days.

Knowing what to keep at the end of your creative exercise is important too. What information is critical? What can you afford to lose? Were you expected to deliver a customer-ready solution or the gist of a new concept? And how will you share the eventual solution? In all cases, what you choose to keep is of best value when it describes a complete, cohesive story. A complete story describes the solution, how it was developed and why it is appropriate. It also describes why some other options were rejected.

Creativity is an exciting process of discovery. Setting some limits on your limitless thinking will give clear direction to that process. Limits do not inhibit creative thinking—limits enable it.

TRUTH

23

Different starting places lead to different results

You might already be aware that there is a massive creativity chasm between organisations and their customers. Customers do cool, investigative, socially linked things to find out about goods and services. Organisations tend to adhere to what they have always done.

Customers are embracing tools like social networking and accessing information from a variety of sources. They are behaving like tribes— forming and reforming as the needs appear. They are well armed, mobile and in control. They are highly creative in what they review and buy. They are demonstrating their collective power, leaving sellers in no doubt about the need to produce good products or face extinction.

On the organisation side of this equation, customer response processes have hardly changed for most companies. Customers are assumed to behave like neatly arranged market segments while strategy still emerges from anodyne planning programmes. Companies dust off last year's strategy, improve the targets by 10 per cent, give it a catchy mission statement and ship it out as a new direction. A new service is conceived and then routinely tested in focus groups

> Even great ideas have trouble surviving in an organisation that behaves in an out-of-date way.

until enough customers say "yes" or "maybe". Where is the creativity? Even great ideas have trouble surviving in an organisation that behaves in an out-of-date way. If your organisation sounds like this, how do you think it will ever keep pace with the creative outlook that your customers have?

The good news is that you can show your organisation how to use creative approaches that tap into the sort of tribal, well-armed thinking that individuals are applying. You can help them to start from a different place in order to get different results. Below are six different starting points to think on. Each is a creative way for you and your organisation to actively engage with your customers.

Customer attachment

Customer attachment is about how you structure relationships. Individuals, or teams inside your organisation, personally oversee service to selected customers. Attachment is not the same as account management in a sales team. Account managers tend to sell to customers. Attached staff are instead focused on learning from and sharing with their customers. They:

- learn what their customer does;
- learn about how their customer's needs are met by your organisation;
- spend time with their customer, building a close relationship;
- keep notes about their customer's exchanges with your organisation.

Attached staff are given the time and space necessary to feed back their fresh insights. What soon develops is a network of people with intimate knowledge of your organisation's customers.

Shop floor learning

Shop floor learning gets your organisation back in touch with day-to-day customer activity. It involves regularly getting desk-bound office staff out to shops, call centres or other customer touch points. Remote staff experience customers at first hand, get exposed to customer needs and see how staff at the front line meet those needs. Insights gained from the shop floor should help to build creative solutions that meet real customer needs. Regular visits will keep desk-bound decision-makers in tune with the current needs of customers and of staff on the front line.

Contrarian views

Every movement has a counter-movement. Popular opinion is usually a pretty good indicator of the mood of here and now. But popular opinion may not always be enough. Contrarians can be helpful here. Contrarians maintain different perspectives. They do this with

But popular opinion may not always be enough. Contrarians can be helpful here.

gusto. They have to, because they represent not just a minority perspective but an altogether different stance. Engaging with contrarians—appreciating their passion, even if you disagree—is a great way to open your mind to interesting points of view and to make new creative connections.

Co-created stories

Everyone loves a good story. Just think of a favourite book or film. Customers who use the products and services of your organisation have stories to tell too. They can talk about characteristics that they value most and how your goods are special to them. Patagonia and W. L. Gore are examples of organisations that appreciate the power of creating stories with their customers.[1] Introduce your organisation to these customer stories. Then create more stories alongside customers. These can be used to communicate key messages to the outside world. They can also be used internally to try out new customer ideas or to keep alive a spirit of innovation.

Fringe groups

Sometimes, customers use products in ways that were not intended. A fringe group develops when reasonable momentum forms behind these unintended uses. HOPE, for instance, is an interesting fringe group that technology firms might want to pay heed to. HOPE stands for Hackers On Planet Earth and these guys have some specific and sometimes leading-edge expertise. Engaging with fringe groups, much like contrarians, gives you exposure to new points of view. Sometimes, fringe group uses are actually early signs of entirely new areas developing (see the skateboarding example in Truth 9).

Games

Interactive games are a good way to learn about how others see the world.

For example, I once worked with a group who wanted to know more about listening to customers. I told them that I had invited a pair of consultants to the office who had years of experience. I turned up the next week with two children and two copies of the PC game, *RollerCoaster Tycoon*.[2] I divided the group into two teams, assigned a child (as adviser) to each team and asked them to build the best theme park possible.

One team focused on things like optimal ride times, maximum seating and cost per ride. The second team learned to "click" on customers and seek their opinions. It was the second team who won. Their customers were more satisfied and their park was more successful. Both teams learned to challenge their assumptions about decisions they were taking and on who the experts really were. It was a fun and unforgettable way for them to learn about maintaining customer focus and to check their theories on expertise.

Bridging the chasm between creative individuals and lethargic organisations is important if you are to provide ideas that are meaningful and relevant. The approaches above can help your organisation to work with its customers in innovative and knowledge-forming ways. And you can start things rolling.

TRUTH

24

Your creativity budget can be
less than £10

During years of good performance, creativity provides a competitive edge. It mobilises a workforce, keeps inspirations flowing and refreshes your strategic direction. Creativity can be even more important during lean years. It can revitalise staff and give your organisation a virtual lifeline. It can make the difference between profit and loss. If only everyone recognised its ability to build solidarity and generate opportunities.

As creativity remains an enigma to some people, you will need to be prepared to defend your creativity budget. You should know how you will measure success and keep a record of your creative output. Truth 17 discusses the business planning behind creativity and some key measures that might be important.

There is something else you can do. You can keep your creativity budget low. Very low. You may even be able to keep your creativity budget under £10. That is less than the boss's lunch.

Keeping your budget low should not affect the quality of your creative work. You just need to bear in mind some core ingredients. A recipe for creative working looks like the following.

> Keeping your budget low should not affect the quality of your creative work.

- **Engagement**—How you work needs to capture hearts and minds.

- **Interaction**—Your colleagues need to feel it and touch it. They need to know that they are having an influence, by participating. In good times and bad, a creative process can help people to feel valued, upbeat and connected.

- **Flexibility**—What you use, how it is used and who uses it needs to cater to a wide variety of people.

- **Visibility**—Whatever you do, let your work be seen.

Below are three suggestions for combining these ingredients into inexpensive creative programmes. Each costs less than £10, which should keep you off the radar of the budget cutters. And nowhere is quality compromised for cost.

Roadmap to the future

Imagine a large wall space in a well-travelled part of your organisation. Now imagine that on it is a roadmap that leads to where your organisation wants to be. At one end is now. At the other is your company's vision. Between the two are five to ten key strands that are important to your organisation. These could be functions like marketing, or areas of specific emphasis like growth and brand.

The route between now and the future is populated with sticky notes. On each is a statement about what must happen. It is a collection of items and resources that are *within your control* as an organisation. The sticky notes can be placed by anyone. They can be rearranged. With time, some will get replaced with real happenings—items that represent progress. These might be quotes from the CEO, products that have been launched or key results. The thoughts quickly become a roadmap to the future. People can readily see the wishes of the past becoming reality. They can see where things stand. Most of all, they are aware that they and their colleagues have built the roadmap between them.

Resources: *A big wall space and sticky notes.*

Trends and insights

Imagine the same wall space, or one nearby. This time the sticky notes are about *external* issues that may affect where your organisation wants to go, but *where you have no control*. Between now and a set time in the future are at least five strands of influence—societal, technological, economic, environmental and political (known as STEEP).

Like the roadmap to the future, the wall is accessible to anyone. They use sticky notes to record insights and possible drivers of change. An insight occurs when someone reads an article, discusses a topic or sees a programme and it sparks a thought that could affect your organisation. Insights that feel more heavyweight or impactful are drivers. Finally, records of real events are added to the wall. These are actual articles that bring home a particular point. These help to solidify the insights and drivers and to give real meaning to the collection of thoughts.

For example, an article on boys' names in the UK can illustrate the driver of increased cultural diversity in Britain. Jack, Joshua, James and Oliver have, for a long tiime, been at or near the top of boys' names given at birth. Muhammad has featured about twentieth on the list over the past few years. However, when you combine the different spellings of Muhammad, it finishes at number two.[1] This is a striking signal of how influences might be changing in the UK.

Soon you will have a healthy group of external factors to address creatively—all built by individuals in your organisation.

Resources: *A big wall space, sticky notes, articles, scissors and a roll of tape.*

Thought board

A thought board is a large canvas where insights and even random thoughts are gathered, graffiti-style. This space is less structured than the previous two. For instance, you might start off a thought board simply by writing down the core values of the company. Then you could ask "What do these mean to you?" Soon, the board will be filled with comments about the meaning of the values and of the values in action. You could post other prompts too. Seeking views on current events, world issues, product critiques and other topics are all fair game on a thought board.

For example, in the exhibition space at Shakespeare's Globe sits a magnetic board. On it are magnets, each with a word written by Shakespeare. Visitors are invited to play with the words. They make their own phrases. This is an ideal use for a thought board. Shakespeare's works were never meant to be studied at a desk in an English class—they were meant to be experienced and enjoyed.

Resources: *A roll of paper and a pen.*

There is one more thing to bear in mind when keeping the budget-bashers away. Try to get creativity used at the front-end of your organisation's processes. Creative involvement early on in the process could provide valuable steerage. You could save a lot of time and

> Creative involvement early on in the process could provide valuable steerage.

money that would have been wasted on developing the wrong concept. Even if you save just one project from heading off into Nowhere Land, you would be demonstrating desired and measurable gains from your creative efforts.

TRUTH

25

Embrace nephelococcygia

If you have never come across the word nephelococcygia before, it means cloud watching. Remember cloud watching? You look at shapes in the sky and notice how they remind you of other things. "There's a snake. That one's a bicycle." Then, in a whiff of wind, your cloud is transformed into something completely different and you see it anew. Cloud watching is expansive, imaginative and ever changing. Creative thinking can be a lot like cloud watching. You should be able to see things in one way and then be prepared to see them in a completely different way moments later. This ability allows you to expand your thoughts so that you can develop the best possible creative answer.

There are a number of ways to consider new angles and find liberating insights that make your solution even better. Let's look at a few.

Delight them

While using this view, you need to go beyond phrases like "meeting customer needs" or "best overall solution". Delight is a perspective where you imagine giving your audience immense satisfaction. Try to build a solution that would make your customers so happy that they tell all their friends about your product. What if your customers liked your goods so much that they became unofficial salesmen? Think about Apple's customers. Are they just customers, or motivated fans?[1]

> You need to go beyond phrases like "meeting customer needs" or "best overall solution".

Below is the text of a real job advertisement seen in a newspaper. It really stood out and looks like they had delight in mind when it was written:

www.upandcomingwebgurufunkadeliccreationsthefutureisasparkin yourmind'seyeyouwanttheworldtoseeitrockthemtotheirbootsitstim eyoulivedthedream.com.[2]

Ease their pain

The opposite view to delight is to locate key moments of pain. Washing the dishes. Traffic. Train delays. Airport security queues. These are some common painful points that are regular whinges wherever you go. Locate the key painful moment for your issue and then start to address it.

For example, a lot of people dread washing the dishes. It feels like wasted time. However, just by adding a radio or audio book, doing the dishes can become special "me time" for some people. The pain becomes pleasure.

Talk, talk, talk

Here your aim is to talk through a process in detail. Appoint a listener. Ask them to take the position of a complete beginner. Then talk them through every single step of the activity you are addressing. This is a particularly good way to think about services and the way you present them. You will be amazed at how complex even a simple task can be, like making an omelette, when you lay out each step.

A variation of this technique is to ask a number of people to describe a single object. The object might be widely known, but its meaning for each person could be different.

A good illustration is this: "Describe a rose." Individual descriptions might key on different personal meanings for a rose—beauty, scent, thorns, planting a rose, a rose pressed inside a book, caring for roses, and so on.

Best possible solution

Think of overengineering your solution. Can you make it absolutely watertight? Use only the best materials and leave nothing unaddressed. Make it durable.

> Think of overengineering your solution.

Maybe make your solution change over time, in line with the person who uses it.

Here is an overengineered pet example. Cats and dogs are popular pets. But as you grow and situations change, a dog or cat is not always appropriate. Can a robot dog or cat provide a similar or better stimulus? You will need to care for it and might grow very fond of it. Plus, as you age, your pet ages too. It can communicate on different levels with you. When you are a child, the dog asks you to play. When you go to university, the dog reminds you to study and then wants to go out for a beer.

Worst possible solution

Think about how to miss the point completely and to make things worse. What if you gave a watch repairman a hammer and chisel as his only tools? What would happen? What would he be forced to do next?

Impossible dream

Ignore convention. Turn the existing view completely on its head. (Those upside-down squeeze bottles in your cupboard are a literal result of this technique.) See whether you can start again and rewrite the rules for how a whole area is perceived. Ask key questions. Why do all toothbrushes look the same? Why can't you have a bookshelf on the ceiling? Do not accept the origins of why your area is the way that it is. Challenge authority. Ignore the laws of physics.

No constraints

What if you had no constraints whatsoever? You have access to unlimited resources. Cost is no object. You are master of all that you see. Now, use your position to make the perfect, unconstrained solution.

Instant feedback

Why not test your idea on real users? If it is a product you are considering, build a mock-up and stick it on a store shelf. Will anybody notice? Thinking of launching a fruit drink? Make a batch, give it away at a music festival and ask your customers whether they would buy it in the future. This is what Innocent did when launching its smoothies.[3]

If you want to test your concept with a lot of people—potentially everyone—put it on a web blog. You could find out what thousands of people think in just a few minutes.

The other guy

Take off your normal hat and wear a few others. How would a man see the problem? A woman? A child? Your parents? Your best friend? Your postman? See whether you can capture their responses in just a few words and then compare between them.

There are other ways to bend and stretch your thinking too. You can always look for deviations, consider the opposite side, amplify the problem, shuffle the order, enlarge the issue or substitute key components. You may find that you like a number of techniques, used in different ways. Or you could become attached to one in particular. The thing is, you won't know until you try. Go on. Somewhere, someone is waiting for you to see things from their point of view.

26

The customer isn't always right—but listen to them anyway

It is difficult being the customer sometimes, because companies are vying for their business, brands want their attention and everyone wants to know what the customer wants. The problem is that a customer only knows what they *think* they want. They cannot always tell you about what they *need*. Almost unlimited choice and various competing messages can make it difficult for customers to know what they want—or need—in a hectic world. This knowledge gap can be a big problem if your job is to provide them with creative solutions. How can you provide an innovative solution, if you cannot first determine what is needed?

Choice and messages

Choice. Having so much of it means that customers can be overwhelmed into indecision or into making bad choices. Since they are usually aware of various options,

> Too much choice makes decision-making difficult for customers.

they can sometimes feel awful after some choices are made, because they know what they are missing too. Having a lot of choice could also cause customers to focus on what they still want, rather than enjoying what they have.[1] Too much choice makes decision-making difficult for customers. Or, as the singer Jimmy Buffett once said, "Indecision may or may not be my problem."

Customers also face being caught up in mixed messages. The consultancy Gartner Group illustrates this well with their "hype cycle".[2] A hype cycle describes the life of technologies through five phases—trigger, peak, trough, slope and plateau. Customers who jump into technologies at the start are said to enjoy a *peak of inflated expectation*. This is followed by enduring an abrupt *trough of disillusionment*. This makes sense. Technologies (and other products) arrive on the scene. They are spread thickly through the media and personal conversations while the story is hot. Customers could be falling for items that they don't really need in their lives— but that feel right at the time. They could also find themselves using products that, far from meeting their needs, just add to their frustrations. Then, when the story slows, so does the media. The product then settles at a plateau point between the peak and trough.

Try a little empathy

What does this jumbled up customer perspective mean to you? If a customer cannot tell you their needs, what do you do? You watch them closely in order to learn about them. You observe moments, look for behaviours and you become empathetic to their situation.

Empathic research differs from typical market research in a couple of ways. Market research looks at a lot of people who, on average, best represent a particular group. The larger the sample, the better the result. These groups can represent any number of customer segments, such as middle-aged men, young professionals or ageing baby boomers—the choices are endless. Using the findings of the study, an idea is formed and a resultant product or service emerges. Basically, by looking at a lot of similar people, one key idea emerges.

In contrast, empathic research needs only a small number of people. A sample size of less than ten is fine. Further, the people in the sample occupy extreme positions, not an average one. There might be a high-volume user, a diehard fan or maybe someone who does things their own way by using a homemade solution. In empathic research you try to locate the reasoning behind their actions. Then you develop these observations into insights. Lots of them. Each of the insights has potential to become a more complete solution, once you start to evaluate them.

> In empathic research you try to locate the reasoning behind their actions.

In a nutshell:

- market research is a process of reduction, from hundreds of people stating explicit, current needs, down to one or two ideas that seem to have the greatest merit;

- empathic research is an expansive process of studying a few people in-depth to develop a number of insights about unexpressed or latent needs, which can lead to a lot of ideas.

Both typical market research and empathic methods are valuable. Using the two together to complement each other is more valuable than either method on its own. The key is for you to recognise the different perspectives that each brings.

Doing the work

When getting to know a customer in an empathic way, a few things are helpful to remember.

- **Try to observe them in their own environment**—At home is good. If you are looking at eating habits, try a restaurant. What you don't want to do is to invite them into your office for a meeting. In an office setting, you are likely to discuss only current needs, not expose latent ones.

- **Listen out for contextual comments and actions**—Statements like, "I am the one who usually organises our evenings."

- **Look for confirmation**—If a customer says that they read a lot, look for a bookshelf (and books). If they talk about a particular diet, ask whether you can check out the contents of their refrigerator.

- **Watch for supportive or contradictory body language**—See whether they do what they say.

- **Look for examples where they have avoided an issue by building their own solution**—A piece of ribbon tied to a suitcase might be an expression of a latent need for identifiable, personalised luggage.

The overall process of researching in an empathic way is to observe, draw insights and convert these insights into ideas. Should you need any help in your empathic work, look for organisations who specialise in it—ethnographic researchers, sociologists, psychologists and cool hunters (trendspotters) are just a few.

Here is a great example of observing and using what people do over what they say. A friend of mine was in charge of a call centre. Her hiring process for new customer service staff was comprehensive and lasted almost a full day. Candidates would be subjected to interviews, live call listen-in sessions, non-live test calls, a questionnaire and a group conversation over tea and biscuits. All other things being equal, do you know who she hired each time? The candidate who poured tea for the others. Obvious, of course, but only when you think empathically about the characteristics that will best serve call centre customers.

TRUTH

27

Complete the pattern and you will find the answer

As a university student, I recall seeing some maintenance workers on the balcony of a building. They were watching people in the square below. A week or so later, I saw the same workers building a new concrete path in the square. They placed it where a worn grass path had existed before. Then it dawned on me. They had observed people's shortcuts through the grass to determine where to place new paths. They were looking for patterns.

Completing patterns is a great way to find creative connections that lead to new solutions. Start with observing patterns to uncover information and identify common attributes. Then draw inferences on what you see. What are the implications of the pattern? What components will cause it to continue? To cease? Once you appreciate the issues, you can design creative solutions. Patterns are all around you and can exist in various forms.

> Completing patterns is a great way to find creative connections that lead to new solutions.

- **Visual patterns**—Just think of waves hitting a seashore or one of those wonderful M. C. Escher sketches like Metamorphosis.[1]

- **Audio patterns**—Music, heartbeats and ticking clocks.

- **Behavioural patterns**—Recall kids on a football pitch relentlessly following the ball or the universal layout of supermarkets to influence shoppers' buying decisions.

Pattern recognition occurs naturally for you. It is why you can distinguish faces of people, for instance. It is an intuitive talent; one that you can easily apply to creativity. Below is a simple delivery conundrum. Try to use pattern thinking to work out your answer:

> Monday to Saturday, each week, a newspaper and the post are delivered to my house. On Saturday the post arrives earlier than usual and the newspaper arrives later. Why is this?

There are patterns in different places—in nature, frequency, recurring themes (models) and in combinations. Each pattern type can be useful to your ability to create.

Patterns in nature

Scientists look at patterns in nature. Modelling the development of cities, for instance, draws from physics. Urban sprawl shares some attributes of bacterial growth.[2] Nature also provides endless patterns of symmetry, time and order. Consider the Golden Ratio and its relationship to proportions in maths, animals and plants and the aesthetics of art and architecture.[3]

Patterns of frequency

Sometimes, you will be exposed to a piece of information for the first time, only to be reminded of it one or more times shortly thereafter. Think about a book recommendation. After one friend recommends it, you make a mental note. After two friends, you add it to a list of books to read. After three recommendations, you buy the book. Think too of the enduring phrases "trouble comes in threes" and "third time lucky".

Patterns in recurring themes and models

Occasionally, you might find some fundamental perspectives from others that hold particular meaning to you. When you spot these core thoughts in a new area, it lends validity to the topic and can help you to construct an appropriate creative solution. Think of Maslow's Hierarchy of Needs[4] and how, as a recurring model, it can add relevance to understanding a new topic.

Patterns in combinations

The arrival of filesharing—the technology behind peer-to-peer communications—is often remembered for changing the music industry for ever. Shawn Fanning created Napster[5] so that he could share music with his friends. In no time at all, thousands were using the technology—millions at its peak.[6] In fact, it was actually the maturing combination of three technologies and some related user behaviour that shook up the music industry. These were:

■ increasing levels of broadband usage;

■ expanding PC storage capacities;

■ peer-to-peer communication.

The three together created an environment for change. Broadband, instead of dial-up, internet access created a usage profile of "all you can download" among users. Substantial PC storage meant that large numbers of big files, such as music, could be easily stored without crashing your PC. And Shawn Fanning's original software provided the catalytic event that brought these technical capabilities and human desires together.

Using patterns

Patterns are used for a number of tasks, such as medical diagnostics, image or character recognition, and creditworthiness—for example, the likelihood of a person to pay their bills. Locating a pattern in your creative work could help you to solve your immediate issue, consider other, related components and provide a possible way to continually assess the issue over the long term.

Patterns are used for a number of tasks.

You can use patterns in another way too. You can imagine a future situation that you want to see occur. Then break it down into its component parts—what must be in place to make this event a reality? These components are the elements of your pattern. When they are all in place, your event is ready to occur.

For example, central locking is common in most new cars. This has been the case for some time. Yet, central locking is not prevalent when it comes to your home and office. Why not? The success with locking cars shows that there is customer acceptance of the concept. What elements of the pattern are outstanding for homes and offices? Here is another example. The paperless office has been discussed as a concept for decades. Numerous support technologies have been available for some time. Why is the concept not yet a reality? What elements of the pattern are still missing?

Before you tackle the larger tasks of central locking and the paperless office, let's return to the simple pattern problem introduced on page 132. Did you work out the reasons for the different Saturday deliveries of the newspaper and post?

The newspaper is delivered by a schoolgirl. With no school start times, she sleeps in on Saturdays and the paper arrives late. The post arrives earlier because the postman is eager to start his weekend—as soon as he finishes his Saturday deliveries.

Any creative solution, to improve weekday post and weekend newspaper delivery times, needs to consider the behaviour patterns of the people doing the jobs. Likewise, creative solutions that you apply to any problem should embrace patterns that you see along the way.

TRUTH

28

The best offence is a good defence

Preparedness is a part of life. When you do it effectively, it improves your chances of success. It is the strength you draw on to face the unexpected. Preparedness is integral to creativity too. Even if you are the most creative person in your office, your ingenuity can still be affected by the slow responses of others, poor odds and things that are not in your control.

As Mr or Mrs Creative at work, you might find the following:

- Not everyone will ask for your involvement.

- Some won't value creativity.

- The topic is open to interpretation.

- Your organisation may not be able to implement creative solutions.

- You will have critics as well as fans (but probably lots more fans).

Dealing with these issues will sometimes require advance preparation. The best approach is a well-planned, preventative action that saves you time, gets you results and maintains control. Below is a list of some preparative steps that you can apply to creativity, which have been divided into three areas.

- Personal creative preparation.

- Preparation for a creative session.

- Ongoing preparation.

Personal creative preparation

Rules of thumb—Learning and applying rules of thumb is effort saving. When you try something new, you can rest assured that somewhere, someone will know a good rule of thumb to assist you. Comfortable stair design, for example follows a rule of thumb of 2 × Riser + Run = 24 to 25 (inches). "Bend your knees" is a common rule of thumb for many sports, and there is a knack to learning poetry.[1]

> Learning and applying rules of thumb is effort saving.

Don't go it alone—There is no reason why you should be on your own in your creative quest. Look around for supporters in your organisation who will take the journey with you.

Use experts—There might be moments where you feel out of your depth, or where a particular focus is needed. If so, get help from an expert. You cannot be expected to know everything and you should not always rely on someone helping you out as a favour. Know what you are good at or capable of doing. Get help for the rest.

Balance the load—You can't be on creative tenterhooks from dawn to dusk. Do other things as well. Try kayaking, enjoy a film or see your family and friends.

Keep asking questions—Curiosity may have killed the cat, but it is a fairly certain bet that he was a lot more insightful and creative before he died. Asking questions while retaining an open mind is the backbone of creativity.

Know the networks—Every organisation has a number of informal networks like personal assistants, smokers, cyclists, maintenance crews and caterers. These (and other) informal groups represent particular points of view and, at times, can carry a lot of weight in the organisation. Get to know them and how they work.

Preparation for a creative session

Rehearse—Know your topic and have a view about where your creative work might take you. Are there particular directions you think you will need to explore? Remember Henry de Bracton's sage advice[2] (which Benjamin Franklin recalled): "An ounce of prevention is worth a pound of cure."

Show intent—Give signs of what you want to do and how you want to incorporate creativity into your work. It is no different from adjusting the rear-view mirror before taking a driving test. It shows the instructor that you are aware of the importance of looking at the road and traffic behind you.

Get in the mood—For the rare times when you are not eager for some creative thinking, try to jump-start the process. Play some music. Treat yourself. Sit somewhere different.

Right tools—Make sure that you have tools around you such as sticky notes, large pieces of paper, a comfortable chair, research documents—whatever you think is appropriate. Then use them.

Use all the senses—Touch, feel, sight, sound and taste. If you can use all the senses in your creative sessions you will see a broader picture and appeal to a wider audience.

Remember good practice—Pay attention to the good practice of others. Benchmark other creative efforts. Pay heed to other people investigating your topic too.

Involvement—Getting people engaged in your activity is always good. Seek contributions—and make it fun. Paint a common picture. Provide a quiz.

External perspectives—Bring in people who have particular points to make on your topic. Having a few specific perspectives could broaden your insights overall.

Ongoing preparation

Shout about it—Help people to know about your creative successes. Tell them. Show them. Teach them.

Be a host—Position yourself as a host for other meetings, where you add creativity to otherwise straightforward and maybe even dull sessions. Be a creativity hub.

Be a creativity hub.

Biscuit tin—Most office teams have a biscuit tin. Make sure that you do and that your biscuits can compete. Ask a biscuit lover for his opinion on how to make your tin more desirable.[3]

Unique feature—Is there something that your space can have that is unique among the rest of the office and that attracts people to your area? A bonsai tree? A recycle point? A fountain? Write-on windows?

Photo spot—Bosses always love to have their photo taken in an interesting setting. What if you had the best setting in the office? When your bosses want a photo opportunity for the press, they will come to your area.

Gimmicks—Don't be afraid to display a gimmick or two, if it gets people involved. Ronald Reagan had red, white and blue Jelly Belly[4] sweets at his inauguration. Sweets, puzzles and games always attract attention.

Change the setting—Rearrange your furniture, rotate your artwork and reinvent your space to keep people interested in your activities. Getting their attention is the first step towards engaging them in your work.

Each of the preparation tips above will help you to bring about creative success. By all means, be creative in the actions you undertake. But remember that good preparation can remove unwanted clutter right at the start.

TRUTH

29

Don't forget the obvious

Creativity is an expansive concept. Occasionally, however, you could find yourself in a very different position, where an obvious solution is staring you in the face.

Look at the list of obvious outcomes below:

- A retractable roof—enabling the use of a stadium in all weather conditions.

- Chocolate and vanilla ice cream—regardless of other flavours, these two are 'must haves' on a dessert menu.

- Shopping—what people will do with their spare time when stranded at airports and waiting for a flight departure.

These three outcomes are very different but each is obvious. You should feel comfortable to progress an obvious solution with your colleagues. Start by addressing a few questions.

If your solution to an issue is obvious, how did the issue come about? Knowing how a situation came to be is helpful for taking the right kind of steps towards resolution. Truth 10 discusses four specific situations where, by challenging the rules about accepted thinking, you might land upon an obvious result.

> Knowing how a situation came to be is helpful for taking the right kind of steps towards resolution.

Should you suggest an obvious solution to your manager? If you have an appropriate solution and if you have exhausted the other alternatives, then yes, your obvious solution is as valid as any.

Will it make you look silly because the answer is not new and innovative? No, of course not. But obvious solutions need good explanation and analysis if you are to convince others of their merit. Your evaluation should progress in the following way.

1. Be cautious of popular opinion.

2. Avoid periphery distractions.

3. Locate the essential elements.

4. Build a system and test it.

5. Demonstrate with models and measure your results.

Let's have a closer look at these steps, using an individual and a team-based example throughout each step—*a dash for cash* and *the case for space*.

Step 1—Be cautious of popular opinion

Popular opinion may suggest that your obvious solution is a non-starter. The people concerned will have grown used to avoiding the problem, leaving it for someone else. They may also be convinced that no one will support an obvious solution—even yours.

■ *Example 1—a dash for cash*: A friend has costs that are spiralling out of control. They seem oblivious to their predicament and are happy to budget in line with past plans. You clearly see that the funding gap will only get worse.

■ *Example 2—the case for space*: You recognise that available space in the organisation is woefully underutilised. Others are complaining about a current lack of space. They are waiting for someone else to reach a decision.

Step 2—Avoid periphery distractions

The situation may be hidden behind one or more periphery topics—the means that others use to dodge the issue. Avoid these. You must identify and focus on the core of the obvious answer.

> You must identify and focus on the core of the obvious answer.

■ *Example 1—a dash for cash*: Your friend can either significantly lower costs or raise income. Obvious solutions. Time and resources spent anywhere else could be a wasted opportunity.

■ *Example 2—the case for space*: People and furniture need to be rearranged, or the space needs to be renovated. A final option is complete relocation.

Step 3—Locate the essential elements

Break down your obvious solution into essential elements. Understand how these elements form a system of related components. Make the essential elements and the resulting system clear.

- *Example 1—a dash for cash*: You build a case for where potential savings can be made—eating out, clothes, furniture, rent, travel, interest charges, and so on. You demonstrate income opportunities and their likelihood for your friend—more pay, changing jobs, a second job, a loan, and so on.

- *Example 2—the case for space*: You investigate available resources and awareness of the issue among those who will ultimately need to deliver a solution. How much time, money, commitment and effort is needed? Where are the constraints?

Step 4—Build a system and test it

Remove each element one at a time. Does the system still function without that element? What is the impact of removing each? Understand the relationships, causes and effects between the core components and their relative impact.

- *Example 1—a dash for cash*: By significantly cutting budgets, savings can be achieved. But your friend will need to change their expectations, lifestyle and behaviour. Tough cost-cutting decisions are needed.

- *Example 2—the case for space*: You (hypothetically) conclude that two options are possible. The first is to use a small amount of available funds to modestly increase space. You believe that this will be an irrecoverable cost if you expand more substantially later. Alternatively, you can rearrange the staff in more effective settings.

Step 5—Demonstrate with models and measure your results

Build working models of each solution. Let the people involved see and feel for themselves what a new solution would look like. Measure your results and firm up your opinions about the conclusions you have reached. Modify your solution if needed.

- *Example 1—a dash for cash*: Build sample budgets. Ask your friend to live within the constraints of each new budget, one at a time, for a trial period. A basic spreadsheet might be enough.

Measure their ability to save, the money saved and their overall feelings after each trial.

- *Example 2—the case for space*: You realise that funds are limited and that somehow, you will have to make do with the space that you have. You identify key "neighbour" relationships to maintain in a new environment. You show rearranged office options in a plan. Scaled-down pieces of furniture on a piece of graph paper may be enough. After, you portion off an area to test the new combinations with staff. Measure the functionality of the spaces and staff acceptance of them.

At some point in your creative career, the obvious answer will turn out to be the right one. This is not a crime. It is a fact to deal with. In dealing with it, just be sure to focus on the core aspects of the situation, model the possible solutions with those who are affected and then measure your results. You should be able to overcome the historic resistance to the obvious and stimulate a willing set of participants as well.

> At some point in your creative career, the obvious answer will turn out to be the right one.

TRUTH

30

Team diversity is a virtue

Having a diverse collection of people in a team makes a lot of sense if you are building creative solutions. The group can draw on broader sources and has greater opportunity to make creative connections. Having diversity is like possessing a bigger brain—the team is able to do more.

Recruiting diversity is one way to assemble dissimilar views. Nurturing diversity within an established team is another. Good recruiting and attentive development keep diversity from becoming divisive. They help a creative team to function as one holistic, dynamic unit.

> Good recruiting and attentive development keep diversity from becoming divisive.

Recruiting diversity

The first two questions to address when hiring are probably can a candidate do the job and will they fit in with the team? Two positive answers is a great start. Going forward in the process, things can get complicated. People often hire in their own likeness, for instance. It is a common problem and a sure route towards unwelcome, consensual groupthink. The issue is made worse if the hiring process for potential members of your team does little more than ask candidates to talk about their CV.

Avoid this trap by using different questions at an interview. Set applicants questions that reveal the way that they think. Later, you can compare their responses with those of your teammates. Ask candidates to describe emotive items like the sea, the moon or a sunset in just one or two words. Separately, ask open-ended questions that call for expansive responses—for example, "What is your dream job like?" Both types of question are open to personal interpretation and will guarantee that you get a variation in the responses you receive from candidates. Try alternating the question types—one- or two-word answers versus expansive ones—to ensure that candidates can think on the move and that they answer emotively rather than supply you with planned, CV-led responses.

Once team members are in place, keep in mind that the different points of view that have been harvested will feed the group's creative activities. Efforts that are taken to avoid uniformity at the hiring phase will bring more experiences, a wider spectrum of thought origins and a platform for healthy debate. These qualities are sound ingredients for well-rounded, comprehensive and creative problem-solving.

Nurturing diversity

Extracting the best creative results possible from a team requires adherence to some basic guidelines, as outlined below.

Complement each other by ensuring that individual differences are known and emphasised in your work together. Never stop observing other members in the team and acknowledge the strengths of each person as they wax and wane.

Encourage co-dependency of the team. Pair expansive thinkers with tactical doers, or natural starters with natural finishers. Always seek comprehensive combinations of skills. Highlight the moments when individuals complement each other's thoughts and how valuable this is as a tool for tackling complex issues. Offsite team days are good for pointing out areas of individual talent and team co-dependencies.

> Always seek comprehensive combinations of skills.

Build and reward mutual trust and solidarity. The team must function well as a unit, but only because each person is aware of the roles of others and has faith that everyone will do their own tasks. Think of a commercial kitchen or rugby teams as examples. Every position concentrates on a specific task, yet each is dependent on the other to do their job if the team is to perform as a unit.

Nurture open minds by embracing new experiences and stretching individual skills. By working on a variety of issues and projects, a group can learn about new areas, develop new skills and see new linkages. In addition, vary the team members that you work alongside. Consider a dancer who is regularly exposed to different partners. Each partner will have a unique style, yet the basic ability to lead and/or follow in harmony is always needed. The two must work as one unit if they are to be successful.

Measures of success need to be clearly understood and actively supported. These will likely be a mixture of performance and behaviour, plus specifics such as using individual talents and demonstrating an ability to adapt to different people, topics and approaches.

Spread leadership around. Encourage the ownership of topics and devolve decision-making among your colleagues. This facilitates sharing of ideas and provides opportunities to build confidence in independent thinking.

Demonstrate the skills, views and collective talent of the team. Show others that the capacity of the group is voracious and adaptable enough to tackle a wide variety of issues and topics.

Supplementing a core team

Even if a bright, talented and enormously creative team of people is put in place, it will still need an occasional injection of additional influences. This will keep the team engaged, aware and stimulated. Think through potential supplemental influences with a similar level of care that is applied to hiring staff.

First, try to think of involving other work colleagues in different ways. Organisations tend to default to staid comments like, "Let's get someone from department x along to our meeting next week." This is good for cross-functional participation, but how does it improve your ability to create? A better question to ask is, "What type of thinker do we need?" Which department they hail from is secondary. Do you want a visionary or a pragmatist? An academic? A futurist? What about an optimist or a pessimist—which would suit the situation best?

Second, use systems that regularly rotate people into and out of the team. For example, people external to your organisation can be invited for brief sessions. Additionally, longer rotations of internal secondment and employee exchange programmes can be set up. Each system is useful for mixing people and delivering new experiences. There are dozens of themes for you to consider when mixing up the team—experience, nationality, perspective, thinking preferences, learning styles, educational background, metier and family position (eldest, youngest, etc.) are just a start. Do not be afraid to quickly rotate talent into or out of the team on an impromptu basis to creatively face an immediate issue.

> Do not be afraid to quickly rotate talent into or out of the team.

Having diversity in a group delivers more, this is clear. As one of the team, do your utmost to make sure that you are a positive contributor and that you help to draw the best results possible from the distinct team assembled.

31

Impassioned people make the difference

If a team is to consistently tackle issues with a creative flair, they will need a stance that sets them apart and the desire to question everything. Call it oomph, pizzazz or whatever you think best. The fact is that they will have to rely on their strengths, be aware of their limitations and constantly ask questions about the status quo. In a phrase, they will need to be "impassioned people who challenge the current view".

Passion and challenge work hand in hand to build successful creative outcomes. People who are passionate about issues and discovering solutions to them are tireless in their search. They are able to withstand hard knocks. They are determined and relentless.

> Passion and challenge work hand in hand to build successful creative outcomes.

People who challenge the status quo are continually questioning the existence of what others accept. They look for reasoning. They want to comprehend and are not afraid to ask—again and again—if necessary. They look for cohesion, completeness and for clarity.

Combining passion and the ability to challenge should be at the heart of a creative team. With these two attributes firmly in place, the team will possess the primary means to consider things anew and, hopefully, bring about lasting, positive change to your organisation.

Passion

The determination and resilience of passion comes from knowing, sharing and believing in what is undertaken as a group. Discussing and understanding a clear direction is vital. Where appropriate, team members can align their overall direction to a campaign as well. Campaigns demand belief and stamina.

Passion in a group has a determined quality. This comes from the team members understanding how they work together. There is faith in the group's overall ability to perform. Ultimately, passion is reinforced and brought to life with results. Successful teams thrive on the feeling of a coherent story emerging and on seeing results that are consistent with their overall direction.

Team members will also bring their own individual passionate topics. These can expand and contract as new interests are explored and as personal connections are made. Individual passions may not seem aligned to the group. This does not matter, they are still valuable. Finding out about individual team member pursuits and encouraging the sharing of this information will build team respect and camaraderie. It will also provide stepping off points towards new creative connections.

Encouraging team members to organise group activities around shared or individual passions provides the potential to build bonds and strengthen the ability of the group to work better together.

A former team member of mine was passionate about food and another about boats. These interests featured in many of their conversations. They were important subjects to each; a way of enjoying life and of making sense of the world. When they chose meeting venues, the outcome was always delightful. For the food lover, locating a new and interesting restaurant was key. For the boater, we sometimes went to the Serpentine in London's Hyde Park and talked while rowing on the lake.

Of course, a little balance is required when supporting passions. By all means, support each person's current interests and what the team is aiming to deliver. At the same time, bear in mind the need to foster additional learning and the development of new skills. If you do, you will be serving not only what your colleagues know, but also what each can learn. New learning and skills ultimately lead to new creative connections.

Finally, let leadership be a characteristic in everyone. Of course, not everyone will want to play a lead role all of the time. This is fine, because leadership can shine through in support roles just as well. How you behave. What you do. What you say and why you say it. Consistency through your words and actions, measured against a common direction, is vital if you want your teammates to behave similarly.

Challenge

For a team to challenge current views, they will need a desire to do so and the freedom to act. Desire to challenge can be inherent in some individuals. Be thoughtful in who is hired (see Truth 30) and maybe you will find that a natural desire to challenge will emerge. Otherwise, be prepared to cultivate desire. Do this by making your creative work thorough, independently minded and emotionally gripping. Thoroughness brings robustness. Independent thinking permits the questioning of authority, of rules and of all that went before. Emotionally gripping issues stimulate a challenging

Make your creative investigations stretching.

response—no one wants to only part-solve an absorbing matter. Make your creative investigations stretching. Push each other for clear, concise and explanative output. Stretch the targets and each other. By facing up to challenges, the team will develop a more challenging response.

Having the freedom to challenge is in part about roles and responsibilities. Each person needs space to perform and to ask questions. Beyond this, be aware that freedom is also about attitude. The team should check its accepted beliefs and query the unknown. Let the new topics and areas that you face make champions of team members. Ensure that everyone is included and be prepared to learn from others. Reward instinctive behaviour. Push back where underlying meaning remains elusive.

Try a format of temporarily assigning the roles of observer, leader and devil's advocate, to ensure contribution from everyone. Attain regular, honest feedback at all times.

The anthropologist Margaret Mead once said, "Never doubt that a small group of thoughtful, committed citizens can change the world; indeed, it is the only thing that ever has."[1] For a team to deliver creative world-changing solutions, they will need passion. They will also need to feel the freedom to challenge. Organisations are typically littered with people—entire divisions of people—who focus on the here and now and on popular schools of thought. So it is imperative that the team that you are part of looks at things differently. Take great comfort in the fact that your team is filled with impassioned people challenging the current view.

TRUTH

32

Reading—your window for ideas

Sometimes, you will not be creative about a subject until you can imagine what it is like to stand in the shoes of others. Getting out and experiencing this at first hand is always best. But there is not enough time and money for every person to experience everything at first hand. Luckily, a ready supplement is nearer than you might think. Reading. It is a great way to multiply the exposure of a team to different concepts, new thinking and greater knowledge.

The benefits from reading are enormous. At a basic level, literacy is key to helping disenfranchised people and developing countries to improve their outlook and opportunities. It opens doors to education and to practical tasks like working in an office. Beyond literacy, reading provides a whole lot more, such as:

- building confidence;
- giving insight into other environments or cultures;
- improving language skills;
- widening topics of conversation;
- showing ways to convey thoughts;
- relaxing the mind;
- expanding imagination.

Reading provides the means to develop skills, bond with others, learn new material and even escape from routine. It is low-cost education waiting to be utilised. A host of studies and institutions, like the NHS, emphasise the benefits of reading.[1] Use it as a powerful way to heighten your personal creative abilities and that of your fellow team members.

The hurdle lies in what normally gets read inside businesses. Much of it is standard fare across every industry—financial news, trade press and management articles. And, of course, lots of PowerPoint slides. The phrase "you are what you read" comes to mind for many organisations and teams of people, but only in a boring, repetitive sense. They read the same material and they produce the same type of results. Where is the innovation and new thinking? How will they see the world from the position of others? How will they see changes coming, and prepare for them, before their competition does?

When speaking to a large business audience, I often ask a few reading questions. "Who reads *The Times*?" Many hands rise. "Who reads *The Economist*?" Still a large number of hands. "The *Wall Street Journal*?" Slightly fewer hands. Then I ask about a less obvious, but relevant magazine for the audience. No hands are raised. The crowd is usually staggered to see for themselves how many people—in all types of companies—read more or less the same material.

It is relatively easy to get reading embedded in a group. It calls for a small dose of process and a little discipline from everyone. Your first objective is to ensure that everyone gets their own benefit from reading. Study deep topics or broad overviews. Look at areas of interest or find bold new perspectives. *Just read*. Then share as a team—this is

> By sharing, more new ground is covered and learning for your whole group multiplies.

your second objective. By sharing, more new ground is covered and learning for your whole group multiplies. Get your team to assign or pick topics for each member. Then meet regularly to discuss the ground covered. By doing this you will get the benefit of new knowledge and build dependencies among the players. Here are a few suggestions for establishing reading as a foundation in your team.

Sometimes, finding **related items** can shed new light. Find a popular topic and instead of reading about it, read *around* it. The emergence of China is a good example. Much of what gets reported in the press is about China as a rising economic power. You can bet that everyone reads this. So why not read around the topic instead? Find out what is under the skin of China's emergence. Will China's increasing influence impact matters like health? Will the world see a rise in the acceptance of complementary and alternative medicine? What about investing? Do you expect people to continue to follow Western investment advice, or will thoughts emerge around investing in accord with the ancient Chinese elements (or phases) of wood, fire, earth, metal and water?[2]

Reading widely is a solid way to get nearer to a number of topics. Each person should be willing to address a topic that they are unused to or that introduces fresh information. Someone who normally reads history can look instead at a seminal piece of science fiction.[3] They may spot parallel themes. An academic in the team can read a lighthearted novel for new insights. Segment, too, by areas of interest; topics that your colleagues want to learn about. Someone interested in learning about drawing will probably read different material—like Betty Edward's *Drawing on the Right Side of the Brain*[4]—from someone who already knows how to draw. Be sure that everyone in the group knows which topic is assigned to whom, to retain that feeling of dependence on each other.

A **book club** can be a less formal way to engage a wider audience. The club sets its own topics and pace. Books (papers, articles) are regularly read and discussed. Reading groups should be allowed to form, splinter and disband, as needed. Comment threads and discussions on each book reviewed can be placed on a company intranet so that others can join in remotely.

Swapping, trading and recycling are dynamic and more random means of sharing. There is no reason why the company canteen or coffee areas cannot have a few shelves of books that everyone can access easily. The National Year of Reading occurred in the UK during 2008. The associated website lists tips for reading, including tips for businesses such as creating a reading garden and converting unused smoking rooms into libraries.[5]

Of course, in an age of mixed media, screens and bandwidth, it would be wrong to discount other forms of gaining knowledge in addition to reading. Films, documentaries, audio books, radio programmes, podcasts and web pages are all excellent sources for information gathering as well. What is critical is that your team has the means to share what they explore, in order to improve the overall learning of the group.

So when you next want to see the world from another's point of view, just read—and share what you discover.

33

Build momentum to bring people with you

Here is a personal question or two. When was the last time that you travelled to work and felt genuinely excited about the imaginative and interesting day ahead? Recently? Are you usually excited about your opportunities to be creative at work? If so, then you are very lucky indeed. You obviously love what you do and do what you love. Many other people, however, find their organisation—and their role in it—to be more ordinary. They see their organisation as a creativity suppressant rather than an inspiration.

Every organisation needs to provide good products and services that people want to buy. This much is straightforward. Some organisations go further. They feel special, cause excitement and have something unique. What they have is momentum. Organisations that lack momentum probably do not even know what they are missing, and they soldier on in darkness. They don't know because they are usually looking for the wrong thing in the first place. Most organisations and their leaders look for something they call "buy-in".

Buy-in is that phrase that always appears in the CEO's speech. They share a new company strategy in a glamorous, company-wide communication exercise and then close by asking for your buy-in. It is meant to create a mood of togetherness. You are supposed to walk out of the auditorium feeling rejuvenated, invigorated and ready to deliver the strategy. The problem is that buy-in is a pipe dream. It doesn't exist. Buy-in suggests that the strategy is 100 per cent right, is communicated with 100 per cent effectiveness and can be carried out with 100 per cent efficiency. This, of course, is nonsense.

Momentum, on the other hand, just asks for the boss to communicate the gist of the strategy, provide a handful of guiding principles (see Truth 35) and then let people get on with their jobs. But what exactly is momentum?

Merriam-Webster's dictionary states that momentum is "strength or force gained by motion or through the development of events". A good illustration is during a sports match, when one team is said to gain momentum over the other. It has the edge. They hold their heads high and stick their chests out proudly. The other team hang their heads and cannot do anything right, and it looks like nothing is going their way. In organisations and teams, momentum is a collective spirit, a feeling of working together to achieve something of value. In some cases, it is about fulfilling a particular stance, like

Momentum turns an organisation into a living, breathing, thinking company.

"make the world a better place". Momentum turns an organisation, from a few thousand separate bodies, into a living, breathing, thinking company.

Consider this story. A Dutch company were in the throes of refreshing their values. Not wanting to lose momentum in the process, they designed ways to get staff to discuss their feelings about the change. Write-on walls, discussion forums and more. One particular method was to give each person a key-ring device. It had five settings, one for each of the new company values. When a person passed another who had their device on the same value setting, they each received a buzz. They could then stop and chat about what the particular value meant to them. Momentum.

Great organisations seem to have the ability to sustain momentum for longer periods. They regularly feature in *Fortune* magazine's annual list of "great companies to work for" or the *Sunday Times* "Best 100".[1] More often than not, a company's longevity as a great place to work is built on more than

Great organisations seem to have the ability to sustain momentum for longer periods.

pay, benefits and perks. It usually has a higher aim, like energetically promoting a unique philosophy or movement. Ethics, authenticity, manners, accountability, genuineness, sincerity, being apologetic when things go wrong and a visible conscience are all descriptions that you might apply to many of the companies that feature on a "best place" list. Could it be that these words also describe attributes of momentum?

Arie de Geus studied companies that live longer than most. He looked at companies that have been around for hundreds of years—

organisations that are not just focused on the short term. What he found was that organisations that last stand for something and act more like living beings than a company only existing to make money.[2] They focus on the organisation as a community of people.

Momentum shares a common thread with the longevity of de Geus' "living companies" and the recognition that comes from being placed on a "best company" list. All three are rewards that must be earned, not prescribed. This is done by taking some decisive steps and putting certain conditions in place. Momentum is earned and really takes off when:

- ◼ straightforward, clear direction is given;
- ◼ key leaders perform visible deeds that are consistent with the strategy and that staff can relate to;
- ◼ people have freedom to choose how best to participate and to what degree;
- ◼ the skills of anticipation and adaptability are valued;
- ◼ there is an organisational *want* to participate;
- ◼ results and key successes help to solidify the strategy.

These conditions are, individually, not difficult to address. Each is achievable with some helpful encouragement on your part. If you work with your colleagues to put these into play, you each have the ability to impact positively on others. When the conditions all happen together, momentum will quickly spread.

Aside from the recognition that momentum delivers, it also provides some practical and welcome rewards.

- ◼ Team motivation is high and people work well together.
- ◼ Management is less laborious, as tasks tend to take care of themselves and self-management occurs.
- ◼ Everyone knows what their role is inside a bigger picture.
- ◼ It is easy to spot when someone deviates too far away from the overall direction.
- ◼ Independent, creative thinking flourishes and is wholly focused on the end goal.

More than just a feeling, momentum creates genuine opportunities for people to imagine new possibilities and to grow these thoughts into real solutions. It makes creativity the rule, not the exception. Momentum is a big stride forward in making your team and your organisation great.

TRUTH

34

Liberate your team with a
shared purpose

With a shared purpose in hand, a team has a firm grasp on what needs to be done and how to do it. The team are ready to explore creatively with clarity and completeness, impressing others with their results.

A shared purpose is sought by a team looking towards each other to ask questions of *who*, *what*, *where* and *why* the team exists. It emerges when the team openly explores these questions and succinctly answers them as one body. In terms of output, a shared purpose is not much more than a single phrase and some supporting information. It isn't lengthy, but it is compelling. It will keep your creative endeavours on track. This is because the phrase is derived from a number of honest, heartfelt and energetic conversations about the true essence of the team.

Shared purpose for teams

The order of events for most teams is to fill the functions, assign a boss and then get going. This might be enough for the group to survive, but it is not going to spur any creative behaviour. A shared purpose can help. It draws teams together to behave as one body, while still making the most of everyone's personal attributes. It provides clarity without imposing restrictions. A shared purpose does not constrain perspectives; it liberates talent. It helps a team to start from a solid base before exploring a wide range of possibilities.

> A shared purpose does not constrain perspectives; it liberates talent.

A shared purpose describes the central tenet of how a team responds to creative challenges. It does not displace personal aims and objectives. Nor does it incapacitate individual thinking. A shared purpose cannot be faked. Team members believe it or they do not. The boss endorses it or does not. It is what everyone in the group believes to be true and critically important.

Developing it happens through conversation. Why are we here? What do we want to accomplish? How will we know when we get there? Open and honest conversation is all that is required.

It is difficult to spot a shared purpose, because they are for team use, not external communication. In fact, an organically developed shared purpose may not look impressive to outsiders at all.

- "All for one and one for all" is famously attached to the Three Musketeers. Its meaning to others is limited, but to the group it was the ultimate rallying cry.
- *Think, Plan, D* . . . (as opposed to *Think, Plan, Do*) is a business example, which described an entire process of a team as instigators and developers of ideas, but not operators. They stopped halfway into *Do*. They also made sure that doers in the organisation were in place and ready to receive their work.

Remember this though—a shared purpose doesn't *have* to appeal to anyone else. The value to a team is immeasurable because they take an explorative journey together. It is their agreed expression of what they are out to achieve. Their very own rallying cry. It can be referred to repeatedly thereafter to make sure that efforts are on track, that emerging ideas are in accord with original intent and that everyone is working in concert.

Shared purpose for specific moments

Sometimes, creative challenges that your team faces will be consuming. Resources will get scarce. Energy will be sapped. And despite the best efforts of everyone, the issues will only grow bigger and nastier. For these challenges, a shared purpose—built on asking who, what, where and why about *the situation*—can help. Specific questions in such circumstances might look like these:

- Why has this event come about?
- Why is this team faced with dealing with it?
- Who else needs to be involved?
- What question is the project sponsor really wanting to address?
- What would a good solution look like?
- Where is the ideal place to find a comparative benchmark?
- Who are the experts that we need?

Answers to these and other questions build a contextual intelligence base, before setting off. This base gives insight into the issues that underlie the problem area and their causes. From this base, a shared purpose for the situation is crafted. The intelligence base is also a place to look for resonance when thinking through creative solutions to the challenge being addressed.

One important point to make clear is that shared purpose is generated from within a team and is not an organisation-wide, autocratic mission statement handed down

Shared purpose is generated from within a team.

from above. Mission statements for the whole company are usually high-level descriptions from senior management, which may or may not always be realistic. Organisations sometimes have trouble living up to their mission statements. Just think of the unravelling of Enron in 2002, for example. The energy business imploded in a very public way, despite having a beautifully crafted mission statement about respect, integrity, communication and excellence.

In complete contrast, shared purpose is created by a team in agreement, so that the group can function optimally and creatively together. It is the qualities of co-creation and belief that set shared purpose apart as a versatile and exciting team enhancement.

A shared purpose is the best way to build solidarity before starting the expansive task of exploring creative solutions. Later, when the team is operating at pace—and time is at a premium—you can be assured that everyone is still working in unison, towards the same aim.

35

Creative cultures are
nurtured, not prescribed

A creative culture is one where you feel at ease to think broadly, to challenge routines and to try out alternatives. It is a culture where you are invited to be open-minded and to work with others who think similarly. This kind of culture helps to breed inspiration and inventive behaviour. Culture, however, does not happen by instruction. Culture develops when desired behaviours become reality.

One dynamic way to generate desired behaviours is by introducing guiding principles for a group of people (see Truth 5 for principles for individuals). Guiding principles are a small number of phrases, derived by a team, that are useful in leading their actions.

Guiding principles

A team's guiding principles describe a preferred environment, out of which sought-after behaviours can emerge. They promote a desired culture while still allowing team members the freedom to act in their

A good set of principles is infectious and can stimulate change.

own style. A good set of principles is infectious and can stimulate change. It can clear up a messy situation in quick time.

One company that I worked with had a history of providing the best call centre customer service in their industry. They were also well aware of a shared purpose, centring on "always over-deliver". Lately, however, the call centres had become infested with initiatives and conflicting measures. The staff felt disillusioned and dispirited. In what had become a labyrinth of rules and hierarchy, they no longer felt able to act in accord with the shared purpose.

The proposed solution called for repairs to two immediate areas and the creation of a guiding principle to stimulate preferred behaviour. The first repair was to relax measures on call times. Call centre staff were instantly encouraged to spend more time on calls with customers. The second repair required improved call centre IT support and system availability. The third action was to develop a single guiding principle for use in the call centres. It went like this:

Our service is like oxygen and our customers die after three minutes without it.

This one phrase made the difference in how work was approached, how staff treated each call and, most importantly, how customers felt after ringing in. Staff once again felt empowered to live up to the shared purpose.

Nature, too, provides examples of using guiding principles. Think about geese travelling in a flock. Individual birds only need to adhere to a few principles to serve the entire flock—namely:

- move with the others;
- avoid hitting adjacent birds;
- take your turn at the front.

Group-developed guiding principles can help to better coordinate the actions of a team, in the same way that geese flock together. Individuals should be able to appreciate quickly the gist of a guiding principle and interpret its meaning for their own circumstances. Take the example of "everything in moderation" as a guiding principle. To one person, this might mean that always maintaining an even keel is best for them. To another person, everything in moderation might mean that an occasional overindulgence is acceptable—just as long as it does not happen too regularly. Both of these users of the guiding principle understand its meaning, yet they have interpreted and applied it to suit their own circumstances.

The principles that your team come up with need to be easily remembered and relied upon by everyone in the team. Limit yourselves to under five principles; maybe 30 words in total. Be descriptive but succinct. Does everyone in the team know them? Do they agree on the meaning of each? Below are some illustrative examples of guiding principles to help you.

- **Ask for forgiveness, not permission**—Encourages team members to take risks and to use their instinct to act. It sanctions innovation and says that pushing the limits is acceptable.
- **No one is alone**—Builds teamwork and instils confidence at all levels.

Finally, guiding principles are not objectives, rules or habits. Objectives are a collection of specific, future events that together form a strategy. Objectives follow a SMART format.[1] Rules are typically inflexible, prescriptive statements that tell you what you can or cannot do. Habits highlight areas of repetition and inflexibility. Guiding principles have a more universal application—without being prescriptive. They encourage personal interpretation and application. Objectives, rules and habits are designed to indicate overall direction and any limits that apply. A guiding principle, however, encourages action by leaving it to individuals to ingest its meaning and to apply it accordingly.

Behaviours

Stimulating desired behaviours is the ultimate output of guiding principles. When guiding principles are followed closely, the sought-after behaviours and culture will occur naturally. From the earlier call centre example, you can imagine the kinds of behaviour that emerged once the guiding principle was in place—namely:

> Stimulating desired behaviours is the ultimate output of guiding principles.

- eagerness to please;
- calls answered faster;
- increased courteousness;
- resolutions to customer issues reached more quickly.

Visibility of behaviours in action can have a hugely positive effect on igniting a desired culture. Some of these actions will go on to be long remembered and shared widely as exemplars of how to work in the team.

Creative teams thrive in a supportive culture, but you cannot wish a culture into existence, nor can you prescribe it. What you can do is use guiding principles to nurture the behaviours that you would like to see emphasised again and again. When applied well, guiding principles can positively infect other teams too. To get started, all that you and your colleagues need to do is discuss and agree on what your set of shared principles will be.

36

New ideas come from new communities

The paper arrived on the desk, "Strategy as revolution" by Gary Hamel.[1] On the cover was a hand-scribbled note from the CEO: "You might like this, or as the box of pills said to Alice, eat me." The article and the intriguing quote from the CEO were both eye-catching. It was worth the read too.

In Hamel's article, he outlined ten principles to help organisations to be more revolutionary. *Principle 6, strategy making must be democratic*, centred on the need to speak to under-represented groups in order to add creativity to a strategy. Three constituencies were seen as particularly important—youth, newcomers and geographic peripheries.

The point is well made. Most organisations have fairly regimented systems for everything. Who talks to whom is based on the process being applied. HQ-based business planners talk to regional planners. Researchers talk to other researchers. Marketing people talk to ad agencies. And so it goes.

> If your team always talks with the same groups, it will hear similar views being expressed.

It makes sense that if your team always talks with the same groups, it will hear similar views being expressed. Your team will also produce similar results—time and again. Let's look at what originality Hamel's three groups might bring.

Youth are usually idealistic, exuberant and eager for change. They are not lumbered down with baggage or last year's thoughts. They are filled with questions and they say what they think.

For example, in one project I was involved in, our task was to work with youngsters, ages 10–13, to capture their views on obesity in the future.[2] Some of their thoughts immediately stood out as important insights:

- "We want broccoli that tastes like chocolate."
- "Fast food—the more calories it has, the harder the food is to catch."
- "Why can't I exercise while I am playing a computer game and eat junk food in the game which looks and tastes like junk food, but isn't?"

Are solutions being developed to meet their needs? Decisions taken today need to underpin views about tomorrow. This can be achieved by including children—tomorrow's decision-makers—in today's conversations.

Youth are expert at providing matter-of-fact observations and expectations. Consider this story, which took place back when only a small part of the population used mobile phones. Charlie returned home after work, but continued his mobile phone call. He plugged in the phone to its charger once his battery started to die. When finished with the call, his young daughter asked what he had been doing. "Talking on the phone," he said. "Don't be silly Daddy, phones don't have wires."

You can also talk to younger employees in your company. Often they are stuck in low-entry positions, get little respect and are expected to pay their dues and follow orders. They do not have a say in key decisions, but it does not mean that their heads are empty. Why not ask for their input?

Newcomers also have interesting perspectives. They spend their first months absorbing information and will frame this new knowledge around their existing experiences. They make connections and put their brain into overdrive to make sense of things.

For example, to the management of one particular music service, having children learn the violin at age five was a good thing. It brought in additional revenue and they assumed that it gave the kids a head start. A new teacher arrived and soon suggested a change. In the youngest pupils, he saw minimal progress, disaffection and high drop-out rates. He asked management to offer instead a music grounding course to the very young and to start the violin at age six. The result made everyone happy. A lot more children loved their lessons and stayed involved for longer, which, coincidentally, provided the revenues that management sought.

Newcomers are not sure about which subjects are taboo, which managers are prickly and which ideas have been tried before. They are fine-tuned, primed and ready to provide you with inspired input.

> Newcomers are fine-tuned, primed and ready to provide you with inspired input.

I recall a new guy at one company I worked for who walked in, ready for our first meeting. Afterwards, he was grateful for the chat, saying that in his former company, not many people made time for introductory meetings. They were just too busy. I asked how he felt about this. "Busyness," he said, "is the refuge of the incompetent."[3]

People in your organisation's **periphery** are a creative bunch too. They have to be because they miss out on news and key events. They only get visited when there is work to be done or they are reporting back on their results. They represent the B-roads on your company's map, the villages that have been cut off due to the new bypass route. As a consequence, they tend to fend for themselves, forced to piece things together in isolation.

Roger, a New Zealander I know, likes to talk about the ingenious creativity of his countrymen. He says it is due to resource constraints and living off the beaten path. Early settlers had to put up with long and postponed shipping times for spare parts. Repairs were often done by hand in the meantime. This attitude of self-reliance continues today. According to him, a Kiwi can repair just about anything with some No 8 bailing wire.

Periphery does not have to be based solely on geography either. It could be that your organisation has areas that mentally sit on the periphery. Maybe some areas make a product that amounts to only a smidgen of overall revenues, or they look after a quiet, legacy part of your business. If your team talks with these people, you can be sure that:

- they will welcome you;
- you will be tapping an unused resource;
- they might have some unique insights from their time in the wilderness.

There may also be other groups whose untapped ingenuity is waiting to be used. How about those who have retired? People who used to work for key competition? Those who do volunteer work in their spare time?

Some of the constituencies in your organisation get more attention than others. This limits creativeness. Find the groups who are sought out less and ask them what they think, see and feel. Then compare these results with mainstream views. You should find that insights emerge in your team, new communities form and your organisation benefits from having cast a wider net.

37

Management tools work, but never admit that you are using one

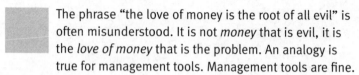

The phrase "the love of money is the root of all evil" is often misunderstood. It is not *money* that is evil, it is the *love of money* that is the problem. An analogy is true for management tools. Management tools are fine. They are necessary, practical and can help to develop resourceful thinking. But the *rather ordinary application of management tools* is the problem. It is the root of alienation and elitism and it can sterilise creativity.

In your next meeting, try explaining tools like business process re-engineering or comparative analysis technique without putting your colleagues to sleep within minutes. The knack is to apply management tools while preserving energetic, creative involvement. Use the tools you need, but give them a friendly wrapper. Make them productive, engaging and creative.

Use the tools you need, but give them a friendly wrapper.

Your first aim is to avoid overuse of TLAs—three-letter acronyms. Actually, any length acronym can be dreary if splayed around too much. The use of TLAs to shield away unwieldy terms is widespread. They litter the business world like discarded chewing gum on a pavement. The website Abbreviations.com lists nearly 50,000 business acronyms, many of which are management tools. Launching a tool by giving it a TLA is going to switch people off, not ignite imaginative responses.

The second aim is to get to grips with how and when to apply management tools. Broadly speaking, there are three types of management tool.

1. Tools that look within your sphere of influence.
2. Tools that look beyond your influence.
3. Tools that consolidate thoughts in either point 1 or point 2 above.

There are many other tools, but most fall into one of these three camps. In fact, a complete management review might involve several tools and look like the following.

1. Review things within our control (or influence).

2. Consolidate.

3. Review things outside our control (or influence).

4. Consolidate.

As an image, think of a well-fed snake, with two humps of expansion between two narrow areas of consolidation. A very happy boa.

Third, try to describe and apply your tools in everyday language. Ban jargon. Entice participation. Encourage dialogue. Stick to the basics. Below are some popular management tools and suggested ways that you can lighten their tone.

SWOT analysis is a tool used to look at things where you have significant influence.[1] It is used as a management report structure. For example, "Get your SWOT reports to me by Friday, so I can send mine to the boss this weekend." It is also used as an analysis tool and is usually shown as a 2×2 table.

SWOT suggestion: Replace the staid list format of SWOT with questions that get people in your company thinking about and discussing real issues. Instead of listing a set of well-rehearsed strengths, ask people to talk about why people buy from you. Instead of listing the same tired weaknesses that everyone already knows about, ask your colleagues to discuss why you lose business. Do the same for opportunities and threats by asking people to recall their best (and worst) customer experiences. Build good conversation, not SWOT lists. Then capture some of the stories that unfold. You will be amazed at the intensity and depth of meaning that they convey.

> Build good conversation, not SWOT lists.

STEEP looks at the environment and external factors beyond your limit of influence (STEEP features in Truth 24 as an example of good value for money).[2] In business, it usually exists as a set of bullet points on a presentation slide, giving context to a decision taken or a proposed action.

STEEP suggestion: Replace the presentation bullets with healthy discussions between people from across your organisation. Invite experts for a given area and a smaller number of representatives from the other four areas. This way the "S" group, for example, will primarily look at social matters, but with a hint of "TEEP" perspectives too. Have your five teams work independently from each other, but get them together once in a while to share what they have learnt. When finished, you should have broad information about what forces are acting on your organisation, insights into how to respond intelligently and a group who are ready to act.

Scenario planning focuses on the uncertainty of long-term future developments and builds a number of perspectives on how the world around you might develop. Unfortunately, it is jargon-riddled. As a result, it can get people too focused on the process itself. Instead they should be focused on the outcome of studying the future, in order to make better decisions today.

Scenario planning suggestion: Bring your scenarios to life by getting people to work with them and to mentally *live* in the future. Do this by asking them to write "A day in the life" account, or create newspaper stories, placed several years in the future. Or create an imaginary family and change them throughout the length of the scenario period. Show how the family members develop different perspectives in each of the scenarios over time.

Other tools might just need you to add casual descriptions when you discuss them to make them more accessible. By all means, use a Boston Consulting Group Matrix[3] or portfolio analysis, but tell your team that you want to *rate your products*. Do construct a Balanced Scorecard,[4] but talk of how profitability isn't the only measure. Porter's Five Forces[5] is a powerful tool for studying market conditions; people use it but sometimes call it Five Boxes (apologies to Michael Porter).

The fourth point about getting the most from the management tools that you use is to be aware of users of them who know how to position themselves. For instance, an experienced Post-it player will know how to use sticky notes in a team exercise better than everyone else. They will apply good writing skills, write with a bigger pen than their teammates and use a noticeable colour. In doing so, they know that their sticky notes will stand out more and probably receive greater attention.

If you can creatively apply management tools and avoid jargon, a few benefits will come your way.

- You will more effectively engage others.

- Energy and enthusiasm will abound.

- You will shift emphasis from the tools and place it instead on outputs achieved.

Most importantly, you will be rewarded with inventive outcomes that you have generated.

38

The joke is on you, or at least it should be

"Laughter is the best medicine"—or so says the old expression. Certainly, many people intuitively see laughter as good for you. Some studies indicate that laughter may even provide benefits, such as healthier blood vessels, improved immune system response, lower blood sugar levels and better relaxation.[1] But what does laughter and humour do for creativity? What benefits can you expect? Quite a few, is the answer.

Humour can:

- help people to think broadly and to be themselves;
- reveal personal qualities;
- assemble new information and associations;
- arrive at unexpected destinations;
- build conversation;
- counter stressful conditions;
- share truths.

A vibrant workplace that welcomes humour is one where you feel free to think broadly and to be yourself. Every day, you are invited to bring a more complete self into the workplace—the funny side. You tackle issues with your logical left-brain and make light of them with your right side. You can use humour to give insights into yourself and to reveal qualities in others. And teams? Well, just when you think you know someone, they use humour to show you a little more of themselves.

> Use humour to give insights into yourself and to reveal qualities in others.

Consider this example. You walk into the office, dripping wet and with your mobile already buzzing in your pocket. You drop everything on the desk and retrieve your phone. It is a text from the boss. He is a workaholic, that man. He just cannot leave you alone to enjoy a quick coffee before settling in. Your face flushes with swelling anger. Then you read his text: "Today is national good looking person day. Send this to someone gorgeous. Don't send it back to me, I've already received hundreds." You break into a smile and feel that you are ready to tackle anything.

Seeing more sides to someone gives you the chance to assemble new information. You learn more about how they think and how they view the world. You learn how to work better with them. You can make new associations, too, from the different directions that humour takes you in. A good joke will start you thinking in one direction and then send you somewhere completely different. Try this line from Bob Monkhouse:

Italians, I hate 'em. With their slanty little eyes . . . No, wait, that's italics!

This tiny joke—thirteen words – fills you with initial worry, increases it, and then drops you safely into an innocuous punctuation zone. A wholly unexpected destination.

How about this little teaser from an eight-year-old:

Q: What do you do when you find a space man?
A: Park your car man.

Even a harmless joke like this stimulates creative activity. It causes you to visualise astronauts and outer space before bringing you down to earth with an image of a busy car park. That is a lot of imagining for the cost of just a few words.

Humour builds conversation too. From a creative point of view, a workforce that actively shares is a healthy, lively one. When sharing inspires a few smiling faces along the way, the lively culture becomes contagious.

Humour is a great antidote to stressful work conditions that pile on the pressure. You may think, "Hang on a minute, it's people under stress and with their backs against the wall who are the creative ones." And many times you would be right. There are many stories where quick thinking and adrenaline influenced responses, taken under extreme circumstances, have produced inventive results. But you cannot build a business by stressing people out— not unless you enjoy employment tribunals. Humour is the legal, enjoyable and enriching way to beat stress. However, humour does have limits when it comes to stress. You cannot always laugh your

> Humour is the legal, enjoyable and enriching way to beat stress.

way out of a crisis. Sometimes, things get so serious that they require nothing but serious consideration. Humour that is badly timed, ill-conceived or insensitive can fracture concentration and even damage creativity. *Sensitivity* of humour is as important as *sense* of humour.

Lastly, there is truth in humour. Some comedy can be far more instructional than any operational manual. Think about the leisure industry. Surely there are hoards of rules about how to treat customers and how to communicate? Yet all of that and more can be gleaned from spending a few minutes with the worst hotel manager in sitcoms, John Cleese's Basil Fawlty. Here he has been summoned to a guest's room, where the guest is unhappy with her view:

> *Mrs Richards:* "When I pay for a view, I expect to see something more interesting than that."
>
> *Basil:* "That is Torquay, Madam."
>
> *Mrs Richards:* "Well, it's not good enough."
>
> *Basil:* "Well, may I ask what you were hoping to see from a Torquay hotel bedroom window? Sydney Opera House, perhaps? The Hanging Gardens of Babylon? Herds of wildebeest sweeping majestically . . ."[2]

The whole production run of *Fawlty Towers* is a small enough vault to be considered essential viewing for every leisure industry recruit, yet is big enough in value to last a lifetime. How about David Brent? Ricky Gervais' pathetic office manager character in TV's *The Office* kept most of the UK cringing behind the sofa. Why? Because his faults and limitations are recognisable. Any real life office manager would dread being compared to David Brent, but how telling would such a comparison be? How quickly would that manager change his habits afterwards? Stephen Fry says this about comedy's utility: "It is easy to forget that the most important aspect of comedy, its great saving grace, is its ambiguity. You can simultaneously laugh at a situation and take it seriously."[3]

Humour is a motivating force. No one wants to work in a veritable morgue. They want to enjoy what they do—work or play. By welcoming humour, you encourage a culture that is attractive to existing and prospective employees. It can smooth over moments of discontent and help your team to work well together to problem-solve. It can even be useful to pass on information—usually in how not to conduct yourself. Humour is an individual effort, not a human resources programme that the CEO announces. It is personal and spontaneous. All you have to do is recognise it in your workplace, join in and allow it to flourish.

TRUTH

39

Deskshare builds mindshare

Someday it is going to happen. Somehow you will make the leap. One way or another, you will find the gumption to trade in your desk and sit instead at a shared workspace. Hopefully you will do this of your own volition—not because someone in the finance department halved the fixtures budget. By doing this, you would be inviting conditions that ooze creativity, knowledge would flow better and you could be more productive as a result.

The **creative** pillar is easy to see. A shared workspace means people working together to achieve a common aim and sharing more expansive thoughts. One group. One aim. Lots of interaction. This is straightforward enough. Many business environments, however, still endorse an old-school view, where *knowledge is power*.[1] Here, separatism rules. People say things like: "My cubicle is my domain. Why share?—they won't share with me." A tidal wave of cubicle life is generally accepted, even though deep down it has never felt right. Critics damn it and satirists, like Scott Adams via Dilbert,[2] show us the ridiculousness of life in cubes and offices. If teams simply sat and worked together, organisations would foster much more inventiveness and ingenuity.

A better flow of **knowledge** is the second pillar. People working together have more opportunities to exchange. Simple but true. People collaborate, spread information and build on it to create more knowledge. You would learn the work habits of colleagues and the nuances of their personalities. There would be a wider appreciation of how to complement each other's skills. What is also sure is that you would have fewer dead boring team meetings.

> People working together have more opportunities to exchange.

A great example is a middling agency in London. The central and most exciting room in the office is a large space with big tables and a fully functioning kitchen (and chef). It is not a meeting room, nor an office, but not quite a lunchroom either. It is a great place to be. It is always buzzing with people working, conversations blending together and platefuls of excellent food.

The third pillar is improved **productivity**. People assume that the current view of sticking people in cubicles is somehow efficient. It isn't. Far from it. In his book, *The Living Dead*, David Bolchover cites studies that hint at alarming results.

- On average, workers spend over eight hours per week surfing non-related websites—that is one in every five days.

- Nearly 20 per cent of US workers send up to 20 personal emails per day

- Seventy per cent of internet porn sites are accessed during 9–5 working hours.

By getting people working together, you will reduce some of the worrisome *Living Dead* activities that fragment organisations. You will build an engaged, interactive, cooperative, informed and more productive group of people. Don't splinter and burn all your individual desks just yet though. Some people may need time to settle in to a shared space. The ability to tune into, and out of, conversations

> The ability to tune into, and out of, conversations develops like any skill.

develops like any skill. Besides, there are still occasions in most jobs where quiet working in privacy is necessary.

Let's assume that you are ready to make the change and sit with others in one shared space. Here are some helpful tips to make the most of your new journey.

1. **The personal space question**—Someone will ask about a loss of personal space (people get attached to their corporate cubicles, no matter how grotty they may be). Explain it in the following way. It is true, when sharing a large space with others, that there are no dedicated seats. Is this bad? Not really. In fact, it is nice to have the chance to sit somewhere else now and again, as the mood strikes you.

2. **Emphasise merits**—Cater to an individual talent—for example, by putting a guitar in the corner. Or serve the whole group by having tables and walls that can be easily rearranged, so the space can be reconfigured as needs arise.

3. **Supply and demand**—It sounds bizarre, but by stimulating the odd shortage you can incur a great result. Consider these conundrums. If you have fewer bins, you will use less waste. If you have limited storage, the group will print fewer paper reports. With a limited number of power and network access points, most people will arrive early to be sure to get access. They will also work offline for some of the day, doing other things like reading and thinking, while their colleagues plug in. Are any of these outcomes bad ones? Do these outcomes hinder or help creativity?

4. **Square peg and round table**—When people sit down at a shared table, they select a position for a variety of reasons. Controllers sit at the head of the table. Latecomers get stuck with a corner and an invasive table leg. The softly spoken sit in the middle, out of sight. Each of these choices is valid at a square or rectangular table. At a circular table everyone starts as equals. No one is at the head. Everyone can see everyone else. At a round table, you can be sure that no one is jockeying for position. A circular table levels the playing field for all, while inviting participation and teamwork.

5. **Double-size it**—Here are some guidelines for preserving a creative aspect in a few sizing challenges. First, watch employee growth numbers carefully. Consider new arrangements when the office becomes less personal and people stop referring to each other by name. For example, W.L. Gore say that once one of their locations exceeds 200 people, they start a new one. Second, when planning creative sessions, limit discussion groups to a maximum of ten people. Any more than this and someone will not get to speak enough. Third, when planning external sessions, always book a room that can seat twice as many people as you have attending. This will avoid you being shoved into a pokey broom cupboard, passed off as a meeting room.

Stacking cubicles beside each other is not going to aid an organisation's creativity. Get rid of them. What people need instead is a way to exchange while they work. Sharing workspace is part of the answer. It always should have been.

40

Everybody has a special place

"My best thinking happens in the shower." It is a recognisable phrase because everyone has a best thinking place. There will be characteristics of your place that bring out the best creative aspects in you. Maybe you have more than one place and use each of them for different types of problem-solving? Two things are certain—you have a special place and it is as individual as you are.

You may not always be able to get to your special place. Having a shower during a client meeting might be frowned upon. What you can do, however, is to discover the attributes of your special place and why it suits you. This is vital knowledge that you can carry with you and apply whenever you need it.

Respecting the individuality of special places is important. "One man's meat is another man's poison."[1] Try to accommodate everyone. Below are some descriptions, with a few specific comments from people on how they see their special place. You might find these to be useful when considering the views of your colleagues about their special places.

> Respecting the individuality of special places is important.

Nature—Nature is wonderful. It is soothing and presents a sense of you within the world. Seeing the stars, hearing leaves rustle, walking and gardening are all good examples. Nature is a great place to be quiet, to be still. More extreme natural locations are also useful. Mountains, for instance, give a sense of infinity, vastness, human meekness and vulnerability. They alter your perspective.

Distractions—Some people must have distractions, while others need quiet. The variance is wide, from public buses on one hand to hushed reading rooms on the other. Some noise, like music or background conversations, can be stimulating. Part of your mind is diverted and the rest can think clearly about the task in hand. Momentary distractions like a sudden sound or people passing by a window can provide a chance to refocus. Some distractions can be intense, such as riding a bicycle in traffic. While concentrating on road conditions, you might find that you can clearly see issues that were once blocked.

For those that need no distractions, timing can be key. Thinking in the early hours of the morning or late at night is helpful. At busier times, just moving to a less noisy location may be all that is needed. Moving away from a busy situation can help you to:

- calm down;
- clear your head;
- focus on the problem;
- work through the issues.

Comfort—Beds and duvets feature here, as do pots of tea. Favourite chairs, jumpers and slippers can make all the difference. "What if offices came with slippers so that you could think comfortably and show others that you are not available?" People can find comfort too from activities, like playing the piano.

Familiarity—Walking to the nearby shops is a thought-filled activity for some people, as is a local park. "Sit on a bench. Feed the ducks. Watch them eat. You could be anywhere."

Confinement—Being temporarily confined can focus the mind. This makes the office bathroom a popular space for some people when gathering thoughts. This is probably an indication of the weakness of offices to provide adequate time and space for occasional solitary thinking, rather than the strength of toilets as creative bastions.

Danger—Sometimes an element of danger can help to push the creative limit. A mountain climber or motorcycle rider is readily positioned to throttle their danger level up and down, with little notice. But thinking while having a few drinks can give a feeling of danger to some. "Will you be able to hold on to the thoughts after?" Intelligence impairment or not, what does happen while drinking is that your usual boundaries pale into insignificance.

Escape—Most special places have an aspect of escape to them. Escape to the countryside. Escape from the noise. Driving alone in the car. Escape has many forms. Escape can be as close as your own garden. Mentally, having lunch on a patio at the bottom of the garden—just 15 strides away from the house—can be as good as being 1,000 miles away.

> Escape can be as close as your own garden.

Therapy—A chance to soul-search can be an uplifting way to start off your creative thinking. "The walks were not to reach conclusions, but as a sort of therapy. I was surprised to find that they became longer and longer, and evermore aimless." Your therapy can be a simple reward too, like allowing yourself to have a bar of chocolate before you start to think.

Tradition—Sometimes a sense of tradition can help to find the right frame of mind. Libraries, for example, are filled with people absorbing knowledge. Likewise, institutions display a sense of history where you can identify with various thinkers and the struggles that engaged them.

Procedural versus expansive—The type of task that you are facing could impact on the kind of thinking that you want to apply. The passenger seat in a car is ideal for some people when ordering thoughts—list-building, making notes and drafting storylines. The same is true for a desk and the kitchen table. Expansive thinking might require something else. "Sometimes at the start of the day, I set myself the task of writing three pages of material by hand. It is a stream of consciousness with no censoring involved. The thoughts run in several directions which I might condense into a point later, if it makes sense."

Discovery—Travelling gives you the chance to see people and scenery. A specific quest can feature here too. "Our family table was one where we would try to find a formula for calculating the number of dimples on a golf ball, or how to cut an apple pie into seven equal portions."

Finally, be cognisant that thinking spaces and activities can change with time. "I think best now when I put my daughter to bed and wait for her to fall asleep. When I was younger, I thought in my car. There I was in my Fiesta, deep in thought and in blissful ignorance of the waiting traffic behind me."

TRUTH

41

Seed ideas in a hothouse to help them grow

Ideas are valuable. Inside the kernel of an idea could be your next product or the future direction of your organisation. They are precious and should be treated as such. In their beginnings, ideas are also fragile. New emerging thoughts can seem foreign to some, though, stirring resistance and causing the fledgling ideas to suffer as a result. To overcome this, you can hatch ideas and get them off to a solid start by using the safety of a hothouse environment.

A hothouse is a dedicated team of people coming together to address a specific problem. The mix of people can vary and the hothouse is usually given sanction to behave beyond the confines of normal processes.

Think of it this way. Under a traditional company project approach—like developing a new product—several departments would be involved, although at a distance. Meetings would be attended, reports would be studied and, eventually, a decision would be taken.

Contrast this with a hothouse environment. Here, select people would be placed together, from within, and maybe from outside, the organisation. They would work in the same space for a concentrated period. They would eat, drink and breathe the question on a daily basis. They would exhaustively explore opportunities, look at related examples and develop solutions. Just as the name suggests, a hothouse seeds and nurtures ideas in the same way that a greenhouse gently cocoons young plants.

The process of hothousing provides many benefits, which put ideas on sound footings and help to ensure their robustness over time.

1. Concepts are richer and are developed faster.
2. A collegiate atmosphere spreads.
3. Valuable experience is obtained.
4. A handover process emerges.
5. Lessons are learnt and retained.

These benefits are outlined in more detail below. Inside each are guidelines to follow when putting your own hothouse in place.

Benefit 1—Richer concepts, developed faster

The intensity of a hothouse environment guarantees that rich concepts will emerge. The team is given the mandate to find the best solution. Any ideas that are put forward receive a serious amount of attention, detailed review and analysis. Compare it to a combination of musicians in a jam session, the rigour of a financial due diligence process or the intensity of a half-time team talk in a sports locker room.

> The intensity of a hothouse environment guarantees that rich concepts will emerge.

The speed of development is heightened because a huge amount of focus is given to the team and their efforts. Funding for operating an individual hothouse should be allocated and ring-fenced from the outset. Normal processes do not apply. Does your organisation take three weeks to approve a purchase order? Not in a hothouse. At least it had better not. Take too much time and you handcuff the team's abilities. Does your IT group frown upon non-approved software? Not in a hothouse. What the team needs, the team gets, pronto. Remember, the organisation has given the team the task of finding a solution to a critical matter.

Benefit 2—A collegiate atmosphere spreads

A magical thing happens in a hothouse. A team is drawn together from across the organisation. People representing departments that usually throw insults at each other are suddenly sitting side by side, grappling with a sticky issue. They might have to endure a moment or two as unhappy cellmates, but soon they are in unison. They do this when they realise that the team is in it together and that they are endorsed by senior management. They build dependencies and trust.

This collegiate atmosphere positively affects a lot of people, but two groups in particular. First, it affects the hothouse team itself. They know what they are there to do and they build the relationships necessary to make the venture a success. They work with their newfound colleagues and call in favours from their network across the organisation. Second, the atmosphere affects the departments who have committed people to the hothouse. They see how the hothouse arrangement might be useful on other projects. They also see the importance of addressing hothouse actions that come their way. No group wants to be the cause for the hothouse to stumble or delay. Hothouses breed teamworking and responsiveness.

> Hothouses breed teamworking and responsiveness.

Specific collegiate tasks for the hothouse team include collaboration, hands-on experimentation, displaying work-in-progress, modelling and building prototypes, mock-ups and samples. Each of these activities relentlessly seeks the best possible solution while immersing the whole team.

Benefit 3—Experience is obtained

The hothouse team is exposed to many new experiences. These range from working practices, to areas explored, networks formed and expert knowledge received. They do this through activities like benchmarking, interviews, conversations and visits with experts in related fields. The team will be eager to expand their views and to validate perceived wisdoms.

They also receive experience in communicating their work. Usually, a hothouse team is expected to report their findings at senior levels. Snippets of how they worked as a team are expressed in the story they tell. Sketches, artwork, idea walls and even scribbled notes from significant working sessions are kept and shared as core items learned. These should not be treated lightly or dismissed.

Benefit 4—A handover process emerges

The team is in position when they finish the project, to handover a well-constructed, robust concept for implementation. Some of the team may well remain in place at the front-end of the process, perfecting any niggling aspects that may arise. Other team members will return to the organisation, serving as 'catchers' who ensure that the integrity of the concept remains intact and no dilution occurs.

Even team members who leave the concept altogether upon project completion serve an ongoing purpose. They become ambassadors for both the concept and the hothouse process. They share the ethos of teams working together to creatively problem-solve.

Benefit 5—Lessons are learnt and retained

A hothouse produces rich material that can be used to record and share the journey taken. Capturing lessons learned will improve future sessions. Knowing the detailed meaning behind a solution eliminates wasteful revisits to the topic. Best of all, the journey itself is shared. It is an instrument used to influence the way that your organisation works collaboratively in the future.

42

Dare to share your creative efforts

While you and your colleagues are doing creative things, it makes perfect sense to share your approach and results with others. Show them how you create. Also show them what you have created. When you do, you will find an eager audience who are naturally interested in creative people, places and activities. When sharing, you will also provide a benchmark for other groups who are applying some creative thinking of their own. They would welcome a chance to compare and contrast methods and outcomes (and so should you).

Of course, the biggest reason for sharing what you do is to get your ideas out and about, where they can make a difference. Sharing should not be the last entry on your list of things to do, either. It is not a last-minute activity. To do this well, you will need a system of sharing from start to finish in your process. Think of sharing in these three ways—**integrate, involve and communicate**.

Integrate

To integrate your activities, you need to link them to key streams of thought and work in your organisation. Your pursuits should be inspirational but aligned. The most obvious way to integrate your work is to be visible in what you do. Let others know where you are and what you do. There is a motto among estate agents that says that the three most important things about property are—location,

The most obvious way to integrate your work is to be visible in what you do.

location, location. A similar motto could be applied to the basics of sharing creativity. People need to be able to find you. Secure the best location you can. People also need to know that creative activities happen in your space. Make it accessible and accommodating. Creativity is an engaging topic and people will want to get close to your work. Give them time, space and energy. They will want much more from you than a notice sheet in the lunchroom. Make the process of sharing vivid, reasoned and enjoyable.

In addition to integrating with people, you will need to combine your efforts with organisational topics too. Do this on two levels—overall and local. Then add your own topics to the mix. The three areas together will make a dynamic platform to stand on and will give you a few immediate benefits.

■ Your work could have significant organisational impact.

■ You will be aligned with "mission critical" subjects.

■ You will enjoy far-reaching levels of interest.

Overall, organisational topics are usually driven by key influential groups. These could include the following.

■ The management board.

■ Advisory groups.

■ Strategic planners.

■ Marketing planners.

■ Project planners.

At a local level, you should attach your work to topics of merit, where you can amplify messages by providing a creative slant. This could include:

■ a list of a key manager's "big five things to address";

■ work sponsored by individual departments;

■ selected operational geographies or regions.

Finally, add your own topics of importance to your creative agenda. These are items that you are eager to delve into or where you have specific responsibility.

In all that you do, try to maintain this wider perspective of coupling your own creative outlook with notable overall and local topics. By doing this, you can rest easy knowing that your work is well integrated with, and complementary to, a substantial body of knowledge.

Involve

You will want to involve people, from around your organisation, with your work. It widens the number of views to weigh up and develops a base of followers after your work is done. Truths 22, 30, 33 and 36 lay out a few specific ways to make this a reality—setting limits, diversity, momentum and new communities. You can also design other programmes to involve the people in your organisation. Shell, for instance, has been operating its bespoke GameChanger innovation process since 1996.[1] It is a company-wide system that assists internal innovators by giving them investment, connecting them to experts and providing general advice. Another approach to involvement might be to provide regular opportunities to hear and discuss important issues. These could take place as seminars with invited guests, round-table discussions or audience interviews with key staff and experts.

Take time to consider the most inspirational and effective way to involve others from your organisation in the creative work that you do. Invite participation. Encourage debate. Welcome new thoughts. Bring innovation to the fore.

Communicate

Results. There is no avoiding it—results are what matter. Thankfully, a vigorous creative process will improve the quality, and probably the quantity, of your results. However, your sharing process does not end when you provide a solution to a set problem.

> You need to shout continuously about your work and successes.

You need to shout continuously about your work and successes. Make it clear to others that you see the value of working creatively in order to problem-solve. Then, make it clear to them where the value lies in specific work that you have done or in work that is under way.

Several tools should feature in your communication plans. Build a website. Consider a discussion forum. Send a regular newsletter. Allow people to opt to receive updates via email or SMS. Feed back information from activities that you host, like round-table discussions. Work with other departments that can help you to communicate your message, such as human resources or marketing. Work alongside other groups who, like you, are busy doing creative things and who are eager to share their story.

Mahatma Gandhi is quoted as saying "First they ignore you, then they laugh at you, then they fight you, then you win."[2] This is a solid thought to bear in mind when you dare to share your creative efforts. Telling them once will not be enough. Tell them again and again and involve them throughout your group's creative process. Make your voyage inclusive. Allow colleagues to discover the enjoyment of the creative side of doing business. Even reluctant, distant contributors can surprise you by becoming ardent supporters. Sharing your work is essential. It is the way to awaken creative zealots in your company.

TRUTH

43

Good ideas need quality, acceptance and execution

"Oh, what a brilliant idea, I wish I had thought of that!" Well, maybe. And maybe not too. Now and again, an idea is uttered and it seems absolutely perfect as a solution. Yet, many good ideas never progress any further. They become stuck in a vortex of inactivity, endless questioning and poor delivery. Eventually, they are destined to gather dust on a shelf. Here, even brilliant ideas become valueless.

For an idea to have meaningful value, it should have a good chance of being usefully deployed. A clear path towards reality should accompany it and the idea should have the potential to effect change. The value of an idea is not just a measure of how good it is. Valuable ideas have three intrinsic traits of quality, acceptance and execution:

> # The value of an idea is not just a measure of how good it is.

$$V_{idea} = Q_{idea} \times A_{idea} \times E_{idea}$$

An idea that has **quality** is one that has been through a rigorous, thorough process. Options have been considered. Boundaries have been tested. Underlying meaning is addressed. Trends are explored. Further, quality means that a fleshed-out concept has been developed from the original inspiration and that it is aligned to a desired outcome (five-minute business planning in Truth 17 can help). A quality idea is easily articulated, uniquely different and completely addresses the original brief.

The organisation One Water[1] has a quality idea. It sells bottled water in the UK and elsewhere. All of its profits go towards providing PlayPump water systems in needy villages, where access to clean water is not available. Water is pumped from the ground by children turning on a playground roundabout. Not only is the water clean, but also it is available on demand. It prevents waterborne diseases and saves time for people who otherwise would have had to walk miles for their water. The idea shows quality by its simple but complete story. One Water takes advantage of a commercial position in wealthier countries, to provide a much-needed resource elsewhere, in a hugely beneficial way, using the energy and playfulness of children. Pure genius.

An idea has **acceptance** when people are made aware of it, care about it and want to see it realised. How much they care is largely down to how well you communicate the idea to them. Is your message personal or generic? Can someone internalise your idea and make it their own? This is acceptance.

Timing is an important part of acceptance too. Even a quality idea can suffer from ill-attention if it arrives at an inappropriate moment. Is your audience ready for your idea? If it lacks immediate traction, are you prepared to keep selling its merits? How much time do you have and how much effort can you personally endure before it all becomes too much to handle?

Supporters of your idea can serve as messengers to help spread the word. Always check for the consistency of content that they deliver and the tone used. Consistency is your best friend when getting your idea accepted by

> Consistency is your best friend when getting your idea accepted by others.

others. Remember that any new idea represents a shift from the status quo and that resistance to change is quite normal for many people. Answer these three questions regarding the change behind your idea:

- Will your idea introduce progressive or disruptive change?
- What are the best ways to inform people about the idea and the underlying issue?
- How will you encourage people to show active commitment to the idea?

Communication, timing, messengers and knowing the type of change required help to win and mobilise acceptance of your idea. Consider this example of Greenpeace winning acceptance of an idea in an impressive way. As fans of Apple products, Greenpeace wanted to see Apple use more environmentally friendly materials. It did this in 2006 by building a website that asked Apple users to send an email to Steve Jobs and to take a photo of themselves hugging their Mac. The movement was called Green My Apple.[2] The response was massive—it was acceptance on a grand scale. Greenpeace had tapped one of the most active customer groups on the planet. Just nine months after the website started, Apple announced a serious, and environmentally positive, change in policy. Job done.

The phrase "green my apple" suggests acceptance as well. It is a good example of the messages that can be embedded in an informative, engaging tagline.

An idea has **execution** when it starts to become reality. All of the hard work is over and you finally get to reap your just rewards. Or maybe not. The thing is, how will you make sure that what gets implemented is not a watered-down version of the original concept? Also, how can you know that the solution will be a lasting one? There are a few steps that you can take to clear the path for others to execute your idea.

- Point out all barriers and enablers to successful implementation.
- Know the effort required via alternative success routes for your idea.
- Conduct an organisational skills audit, even a quick one. Then fill any remaining gaps.
- Give visibility to potential rewards and benefits.
- Identify and clearly state measures of expected impact and outcomes.
- Provide a list of attributes of success.
- Be in a position to articulate what is exceptionally good about your solution. Not reasonable, not average, but *breathtakingly* good.

At first, it might seem strange to boil down creative success to a formula of quality, acceptance and execution. The fact is, these three elements are what are required to get your idea out of your head and into the hands of people who will make it a reality.
Anything less is just wishful thinking. Ultimately, you want success in the form of ideas that address genuine problems with first-rate solutions.

TRUTH
44

Recognise, reward and celebrate for long-term success

People who take the time to recognise each other and celebrate together are more successful. Kenichi Ohmae, the renowned strategist, emphasised this point in his list of 12 successful "do's for collaboration".[1] To be fair, the situation is somewhat self-referential, as success breeds celebration just as much as celebration breeds success. The relationship is a symbiotic one.

Moreover, a group that has appreciation and regard for each other is one that works in concert. They get jobs done and enjoy the shared work and process along the way. Roles are known. Systems are proven. Limits are understood. Success is practised. Performance looks less like individual effort and more like a well-oiled production unit. There are four particular areas where recognition, reward and celebration can enrich your inventive spirit.

> A group that has appreciation and regard for each other is one that works in concert.

- Progress made.
- Successful outcomes.
- Cooperation achieved.
- Outright winners.

Take a closer look at each of these four areas in the sections below, bearing in mind two basic, but central, tenets.

- Behaviour that is sought after should be recognised and rewarded when it takes place.
- When celebrating, everyone should be involved and play a role.

Progress made

As your ideas reach levels of increased clarity, there will be natural points of conclusiveness. Perhaps they follow a stage of sifting through a complex investigation to arrive at segments of clarity (see Truth 18). Think of these moments as *islands of stability*. These are good times to recognise effort made or to celebrate achievement. You can simultaneously take a rest, reward dedication and motivate people. If you are in the middle of a large, lengthy investigation, a day away or dinner out might be a good idea. If you find an island of stability during a much shorter exercise of just a few hours, then pause for a cup of coffee or a brief walk. Each is a reward of sorts. In all cases, it is the progress—the positive direction towards a compelling solution—that is given emphasis.

Successful outcomes

Successful solutions represent the ultimate in terms of progress. Your idea has been developed and put in place, and results are rolling in. This is an ideal time to review accomplishments, give well-earned rewards and celebrate together. When reviewing, try to look at three themes:

- What went well and not so well?
- What was most satisfying and most disappointing?
- What improvements can be made next time?

Focusing on these three areas will build up organisational memory, for you, the people you work with and other groups. The memory that you create will improve your chances of future success.

It is very important in these situations for everyone to feel what success is like. Encourage everyone to absorb what a successful, creative undertaking looks like and to embrace a spirit of achievement. Recognise the formula that brought the success and how to readily retain it and use it again. Tying this learning together, alongside a celebration of the crowning moment, produces a memorable and lasting source to draw from in the future. It becomes an event that is returned to again and again.

Cooperation achieved

A group working together in a streamlined way, with few or no flaws, is as notable a success as any eventual solution. Cooperation demonstrates shared learning, increased maturity and the ability to productively combine skills. Recognition for these attributes is well placed. Reward the people involved and the processes applied, when appropriate. For example, the person who manages a process of sharing information between people is just as critical as the initial "idea team" that gave birth to the new concept.

Cooperation can be recognised throughout a creative process, not just at the end. Keep in mind project milestones along the way. Use these as moments to acknowledge project participants. Think too about important dates for individual team members, such as joining dates, birthdays and personal events that arise during your time together. It may seem insignificant, but groups that take time—even a small amount—to show appreciation are already laying a foundation that can improve the chances of a successful outcome.

Outright winners

There is nothing quite like the edginess that competition brings to excite idea creation. Different groups, subgroups and individuals looking at identical issues and information will return with different insights and solutions. By creating a competitive environment, you will ignite a spirit of innovation.

> By creating a competitive environment, you will ignite a spirit of innovation.

The X Prize Foundation is a leading example of innovating through competition.[2] It sets specific challenges, invites teams to participate and gives the winners $10 million (or more) when the objectives have been met. The competitions range from designing and producing highly efficient, commercially desirable cars, to demonstrating improvements in the cost and time required to sequence human genomes.

Your company-specific competition need not be as extensive as the X Prize. You could create a competitive spirit in a workshop setting just by splitting into two or more groups. You could also try sending out teams armed with cameras to capture aspects of a problem that you are addressing.

Another approach is to provide individuals with the same set of raw materials and ask them to, in their own unique way, meet the same aim—like these university students, perhaps. Each student was given ample cardboard sheets but only a brief amount of time to construct a piece of outdoor seating. The task was purposely difficult, in order to stimulate interesting responses. The winning individuals were allowed to celebrate with a drink and were rewarded by displaying their solutions outside the Students' Union building. There, they could invite passers-by to sit and test the results, giving instant feedback.

Recognition, reward and celebration are elements of a vibrant, able workforce. Use them as tools to motivate, help your organisation to bond, improve performance and spur ideas. Use them, too, as a statement to demonstrate success and how you intend it to stay that way.

TRUTH

45

Creativity—the final frontier

Creativity is so crucial to the way that people survive, so ingrained in humanity, that it may well come to be a final frontier. From a societal perspective, it is representative of self-actualisation—Maslow's uppermost tier of needs. In a business setting, making the most of creative talents could turn out to be the last struggle to stay in front of your competition.

Mankind has undergone several changes since arriving on the planet. For the purposes of this truth, these changes can be described as the following three ages.

- **Agricultural**—Early man to mid-1700s.

- **Industrial**—Comprising the century of the Industrial Revolution (circa 1750–1850) and beyond to the early 1900s.

- **Information**—Probably beginning after the arrival of the personal computer, when information became a key asset, but can stem from the discovery of the transistor in 1948.

This list is a gross simplification, of course, as it ignores ages of early man. It also ignores very recent phenomena such as consumerism and the preponderance of disposability, either of which could be used by future generations to describe (unfavourably) aspects of the twentieth and twenty-first centuries. These three ages, however, do outline how mankind has arrived at the third millennium.

Every age takes humanity in new directions. The first age fed basic needs, the second produced on a grand scale to serve people's wants and the third is increasingly focused on people, their interests and how they spend their time. Each age serves a more intricate and complete human condition. The age that we are now entering is one of recognising and fully utilising talent. It is, after all, talent that created Jethro Tull's seed drill, Sir Frank Whittle's jet engine and Tim Berners-Lee's World Wide Web.

> The age that we are now entering is one of recognising and fully utilising talent.

Welcome to the Talent Age. In this period, talent is king. He who has most is in good shape. He who accesses it and uses it well is even better off. In the Talent Age, it is no longer what you know or who you know that is critical. Instead, it is how quickly you *can* know and how well you can respond thereafter. In the Talent Age, companies still say that "people are their greatest asset". Only now they really mean it. Companies rely on their people to stay abreast of lightning-quick market shifts and to invent new ways of remaining competitive. "Snooze and you lose", says the old expression. In the Talent Age, people are the alarm clocks.

Given the magnitude of talent, it is wise to learn how to realise it and then release it most effectively. By improving the skills of the workforce in your organisation, they are able to make greater, more significant contributions. These increased contributions ultimately deliver more opportunities for success. This is a simple, but useful formula. Realising talent might come from the following three primary sources.

- Formal education.
- On-the-job training.
- Experience.

Releasing talent, however, is much more about putting knowledge and experience to use. Here, creativity is the primary route to success. Creative insights carve out new points of difference and competitiveness. If knowledge is the mind of the Talent Age, creativity is its heartbeat.

> If knowledge is the mind of the Talent Age, creativity is its heartbeat.

To utilise creativity to its fullest in the Talent Age, your organisation must value characteristics that stimulate original thinking:

- How well do the employees deal with complexity?
- How well do they adapt to changing circumstances?
- How good are they at anticipating required shifts in direction?
- To what extent is a longer-term view reinforced in daily tactics?
- Does your organisation rely on the instincts and intuition of the employees?
- Does your organisation value networking?

Working in the Talent Age need not be an arduous shift in the way that you and your organisation think. At the most basic level, you just need to observe the interesting and inventive things that people do every day and then act on your observations. These things might appear insignificant to the people doing them. They are so routine as to be nearly invisible.

For example, drying out wet shoes by putting them on a radiator is a signal. Radiators are designed to heat rooms, not to dry out shoes. What need is being expressed that you can address? How about dashboards that house maps, clipboards and other clutter? The drivers and passengers who store items here are giving you a clue about a need that they have.

Does your organisation have the talent to realise these and other insignificant actions that are happening every day? If so, can you act on them, sorting out the need, adapting their perspective and anticipating required shifts in direction? Can you realise a solution for the needs that you uncover? If you can, then you are primed and ready for working in the Talent Age. Enjoy the ride.

TRUTH

46

Feed your creative spirit

There is no doubting that creativity has an impact on your life. You, like people before you, are part of man's ageless search for creative expression. Inherent within you is a spirit of creativity. The process of shaping your spirit can be assisted by a creative agenda. But the *role* of feeding that spirit is yours. In doing so, you may find that you become an inspiration to others, who begin to look to you for creative guidance.

The new recruit: "So, is it just creative people that have a creative expression need?"

You: "No, a creative spirit is a trait that we all have. We each look after and feed our own creative spirit. We take responsibility."

Creativity that is defined by an organisation will alter with managerial changes. To one CEO, creativity is a process. To another, it is the installation of a new product development programme. To a third, it might be a specific team of people set up to be beacons for the organisation. But in each case—however it is portrayed—the organisation's creative agenda is subject to management decisions. Of course, managers' decisions can be based on evidence or on personal whims—wisdom in creative matters does not necessarily increase with seniority.

As a result, creativity in an organisation can only ever be a malleable, temporary system of inputs and outputs. Whether your particular system is an exemplar of creativity in business or a poorly resourced afterthought, it is subject to change and remains a temporary system. This is neither good nor bad. It just is.

Creativity as a personal exercise, however, is timeless. Applying imagination and seeking ingenious solutions has always been sought after, whether tackling ordinary chores, facing world issues or expressing views. There is always a desire to do something better, faster or more innovatively than before. Creativity is a powerful force during periods of renaissance and enlightenment. Longstanding problems fall away as new levels of insight and understanding are reached. The proverbial "height of the bar" is raised for the next generation. Memorable examples of this from the past are as impressive now as they were then. Think of Newton laying out the laws of gravity in *Principia*. Recall the drama that Nureyev brought to ballet. Remember Darwin's world-shattering insight and the immediate ridicule he faced for taking such an unpopular position.

Yet imaginative excellence is not limited to good times only. Creative problem-solving flourishes equally well during lean periods of few resources, poor economic conditions and lapses in a humanitarian perspective. Consider, for instance, the inventiveness behind individual efforts to survive during the Great Depression. Remember the importance of allotments and frugal, but inspired, reuse of limited materials during the war years. Look at rapid improvements in technologies to detect illness after the discovery of the SARS virus.

In all of these situations—good and bad, global and personal— creativity is sought out and relied upon. It is unfaltering in its ability to serve and problem-solve.

This ever-present creative hunger gives you a chance to see yourself in a new light and to visualise opportunities. Then it gives you the ability to place yourself inside a range of scenarios and to explore available options.

The new recruit: "So, what you are saying is that no matter the conditions, everybody applies the same creative process?"

You: "Yes and no. Yes, because there are some constants in all creative processes. No, because there is a strong individual element. Your personal process might be the same, boom or bust, but it is still unique to you. All that changes are the types of question asked. You can make a real change for your company or your surroundings, but it all starts with you."

Fulfilling your creative spirit, we know to be important. What is the best method to do this? There are a few basic elements that you should put into practice. You need to:

■ focus on the correct issues;

■ make connections;

■ communicate your ideas.

Of course, there are no quotas on additional preferences that you can apply to your own creative approach. It is a situation of finding what works for you, what will help you to work with others and what you need to deliver results to your audience. Many of the possible tools, techniques, processes and elements of creativity are inside the truths of this book. Some will have greater appeal to you than others. Will you align your efforts to underlying drivers or to a common

There are no quotas on additional preferences that you can apply to your own creative approach.

aim? Do you need calm spaces to think or utter chaos at times? Are you more productive when facing a deadline or a dead-end problem? These are all possibilities for you in building your own creative approach. Your task is to review them and to work out which aspects are suitable (or irresistibly appealing) for your own inventiveness. Choose what you need and then apply them.

> *The new recruit:* "Oh, I see. I look at what is out there, pick what appeals and build my own scrapbook—a personal manual for creativity. Then I am sorted for the future, right?"

> *You:* "Not quite. It is more like that Gandhi quote that says, 'Be the change you want to see in the world.' A manual is nothing unless you also act. Creativity is timeless. It is inherent within you. It is what people naturally seek. Humanity always has and always will. You just need to make the best of your own skills."

Creativity, it would seem, boils down to a personal question that only you can fully address. No organisation can fulfil your hunger. No model can prescribe your needs. Having spent your valuable time reading about creativity, it would be a shame if you made no changes to your creative approach. If you just put down this book and do nothing different, then nothingness wins. But if you change something, anything, in order to improve your creative outlook, then you win. The personal question is simply this—what will you do differently tomorrow?

References

Truth 1

1 These creativity definitions were gathered by Patrick, when serving as compere at the inaugural World Creative Forum, held in London in 2003.

Truth 3

1 Brainteaser answer:

   Did you think out of the box to understand the journeys of the man in the lift? The rest of his story is that he is small in stature. In the mornings, he can easily press the Lobby button in the lift. In the evenings, if he shares the lift, someone can press the tenth floor button for him. On rainy days, he can use his umbrella. Otherwise, he presses the seventh floor button, the highest one he can reach, and walks up the three remaining flights of stairs.

2 This story is an abridged version of an unpublished work by Oliver Topley, entitled *Looking Backwards Forwards*. Used with permission of the author.

Truth 5

1 To be fair, guiding principles are mostly innate. Sometimes, an extraordinary, unexpected event can cause you to behave in a wholly new way. Later, this new behaviour—good or bad—could become part of your set of guiding principles.

Truth 7

1 The iBot emerged from the inventor Dean Kamen and his company, DEKA Research and Development. DEKA invented portable dialysis machines, the first cardiovascular stent (for opening and stabilising arterial walls) and the Segway personal transporter. More information on DEKA is available at http://www.dekaresearch.com/.

2 Arup Engineers, Foster and Partners, Architects, and Sir Anthony Caro, Sculptor.

Truth 8

1 This story can be found in various online locations. It has not been possible to locate the originator.

Truth 9

1 Patrick worked for Orange from 1991 to 2002, ultimately as Director on Creaticity. The brand values were: straightforward, dynamic, friendly, refreshing and honest.

Truth 10

1 Officially it is known as the International Shakespeare's Globe Centre. The theatre is a highly sensitive recreation of Shakespeare's 1599 Globe Theatre, sited approximately at the original location.

2 Milk floats are small electric carts, typically used by dairies to deliver milk and dairy products. They were popular in many European countries, but their numbers have been declining for years as people have more options with regard to food shopping.

Truth 11

1 Nigel Risner is a motivational speaker, consultant and author of *It's a zoo around here*: the new rules for better communication (2005, 3rd edition), Limitless Publications: Arkley, UK.

Truth 12

1 Konosuke Matsushita was a Japanese businessman, sometimes referred to in his home country as "the God of management". He was the founder of Matsushita Electric. Panasonic is one of its core brands.

2 Wilson, John P. (2005), *Human Resource Development: Learning and Training for Individuals and Organizations*, 2nd edn (online), London: Kogan Page.

3 Quoted in Williamson, O. E. and Winter, S. G. (1993), *The Nature of the Firm: Origins, Evolutions and Development*, New York: Oxford University Press.

Truth 13

1 Steve Jobs, speaking about Mac OS X's Aqua user interface, in Steve Jobs' Apple gets way cooler, *Fortune*, 24 January 2000. Reporter: Brent Schlender; Associate: Christine Y. Chen.

2 Adams, Douglas (1995), *The Hitchhiker's Guide to the Galaxy*, New York: Ballantine Books.

Truth 14

1 Answer:

So how many Fs did you see? There are six Fs in the sentence. Most people only see three—the ones in finished, files and scientific. The other Fs are in the word "of", which appears three times. It is a regularly used word that you might tend to overlook. Also, the F, as used in "of" is a soft phonetic sound. In looking for Fs in the sentence, you tend to look for words with the hard "F" sound.

Truth 15

1 The fringe benefits of failure and the importance of imagination, *Harvard Magazine Inc*, 5 June 2008 (online edition), http://harvardmagazine.com/go/jkrowling.html.

2 The Dyson Story, http://www.dyson.co.uk/.

3 Stanford News Service, 12 June 2005, http://news-service.stanford.edu/news/2005/june15/jobs-061505.html.

Truth 16

1 Shamanism, Paganism and Trance. They sounded far-fetched at the time, like gifts that three wise men would bear. But they reminded me that there is always room to embrace another technique. A few days after disembarking the ship, I accepted my invitation and volunteered for a Trance session . . . but that is another story.

Truth 18

1 In constructing this truth, the author gratefully acknowledges the research work of Chen-Bo Zhong, Ap Dijksterhuis and Adam

Galinsky, authors of The merits of unconscious thought in creativity, *Psychological Science*, Vol. 19, Issue 9 (September 2008), pp. 912–918.

2 Robert Eastaway (1997), Keep it simple, *Financial Times*, January.

3 To be fair, Jardin's Principle also mentions a few circuitous caveats: 1) It is sometimes hard to tell what is simple and what is profound; 2) Those individuals at the complex level believe that there is no higher level than theirs; 3) You are probably wrong about the level of Jardin that you are at; 4) In order to reach the profound level, you must pass through the other two levels; 5) Unless you have a profound understanding of a subject, you are likely either to oversimplify it or to overcomplicate it. Intriguingly, and in accord with the first caveat, it may be difficult to discern if Jardin's Principle is simple . . . or profound.

Truth 19

1 The Toyota website cites the Toyota Production System as, "A production system that is steeped in the philosophy of the complete elimination of all waste and that imbues all aspects of production with this philosophy in pursuit of the most efficient production method." See http://www.toyota.co.jp/en/vision/production_system/.

2 Toyota website, Vision and Philosophy: http://www.toyota.co.jp/en/vision/.

Truth 21

1 The engineers were paying homage to Scott Adams, creator of the cartoon *Dilbert*, when they named this programme.

2 Amazon has made the act of referrals a commonplace activity with its catchphrase of "customers who bought this also bought x". Epinions.com is like Amazon in that it incorporates referrals. It also includes a rating system of other raters—raters whom you trust, raters who trust you, etc. The epinions network forms a web of trust around a given user. 43things.com is a social networking site. Users list things that they want to do and find other people who want to do similar things.

Truth 23

1 Patagonia maintains a blog for employees, friends and customers at http://www.thecleanestline.com/. W. L. Gore & Associates (makers of Gore-Tex) invites customer stories via its community website at http://www.gore-tex.com/remote/Satellite/content/community/real-life-stories.

2 From Wikipedia: "*RollerCoaster Tycoon* is a simulation strategy computer game that simulates theme park management. Developed by MicroProse and Chris Sawyer and published by Hasbro Interactive."

Truth 24

1 The UK National Office of Statistics tracks names given to newborns each year. See also Helen Nugent and Nadia Menuhin (2007), Muhammad is No 2 in boy's names, *The Times*, 6 June, http://www.timesonline.co.uk/tol/news/uk/article1890354.ece.

Truth 25

1 Kahney, L. (2002), Mac loyalists: don't tread on us, *Wired*, 2 December.

2 The advertisement was for a web designer, circa 2000, in *The Times*. The company was Sony.

3 Innocent website: http://www.innocentdrinks.co.uk/us/.

Truth 26

1 Hollis, Liz (2007), Spoilt for choice, *The Times*, 4 July, http://women.timesonline.co.uk/tol/life_and_style/women/the_way_we_live/article2020778.ece.

2 Gartner Group website: http://www.gartner.com/pages/story.php.id.8795.s.8.jsp.

Truth 27

1 The official M. C. Escher website contains details on his work and life: http://www.mcescher.com/.

2 Ball, Philip (2004), *Critical Mass: How one thing leads to another*, London: Arrow Books, The Random House Group Limited, p. 183.

3 From Wikipedia: http://en.wikipedia.org/wiki/Golden_ratio.

4 Abraham Maslow discussed five basic human needs as a hierarchy, or sequence, to be met. These basic needs are: physiological, safety, love, esteem and self-actualisation. The original article appeared in *Psychological Review* in 1943 and is reproduced at http://psychclassics.yorku.ca/Maslow/motivation.htm.

5 The history of Napster is documented on several internet sites, including Wikipedia: http://en.wikipedia.org/wiki/Napster; and the M/Cyclopedia of New Media: http://wiki.media-culture.org.au/index.php/Napster.

6 Napster is now a membership-based, legal download service.

Truth 28

1 Goodwin, Daisy (2008), A poem learnt by heart is a friend for life, *The Sunday Times*, 5 October.

How to learn verse:

1 Read the poem to yourself.

2 Now read the first line of the poem out loud. Take your eyes from the page and immediately say the line again. Glance back to make sure you got it right. If you made a mistake, try again. Now do the same with the second line. Repeat the procedure for every line in the poem.

3 Go back to the beginning. This time, read the first two lines out loud, look away and repeat them aloud. Check. If you made a mistake, try again. Now move on to the next two lines, going through the whole poem two lines at a time.

4 Repeat the process three lines at a time, then four lines at a time, then five and then six. By the sixth pass, no matter how long the poem, you will have it memorised.

5 Recite the whole poem just before you go to bed at night.

6 Crucial: stop thinking about the poem. Your sleeping mind is very important for memory.

7 The next day, you should find (after a glance at the first line to bump-start your memory) that you can recite the whole poem.

http://entertainment.timesonline.co.uk/tol/arts_and_ entertainment/books/poetry/article4880817.ece.

2 Henry de Bracton was an English jurist born in 1268. See http://thinkexist.com/quotation/an_ounce_of_prevention_is_worth _a_pound_of_cure/208042.html. The quote is often attributed to Benjamin Franklin and his *Poor Richard's Almanac*.

3 http://www.nicecupofteaandasitdown.com/.

4 Jelly Belly is a registered trademark of The Jelly Belly Candy Company, Fairfield, CA.

Truth 31

1 www.thinkexist.com.

Truth 32

1 NHS Choices website: http://www.nhs.uk/Pages/homepage.aspx.

2 Five phases in accordance with classic Chinese philosophy. See also Wikipedia: http://en.wikipedia.org/wiki/Wu_Xing.

3 William Gibson's *Neuromancer* (1995), Voyager and Neal Stephenson's *Snow Crash* (2000), Spectra Books, are two good examples.

4 *Drawing on the Right Side of the Brain* was first published in 1979 by J. P. Tarcher: Los Angeles, USA and is a formative and well-used guide for developing artistic confidence. It winds its way into many conversations.

5 http://www.yearofreading.org.uk/index.php?id=77.

Truth 33

1 Both lists can be found online at:
http://money.cnn.com/magazines/fortune/bestcompanies/2008/ full_list/ and
http://business.timesonline.co.uk/tol/business/career_and_jobs/ best_100_companies/.

2 de Geus, Arie (1999), *The Living Company: Growth, Learning and Longevity in Business*, Nicholas Brealey Publishing Limited, London, UK.

Truth 35

1 SMART: specific, measurable, achievable, realistic and time-based.

Truth 36

1 Hamel, Gary (1996), Strategy as revolution, *Harvard Business Review*, July–August.

2 Patrick worked with the UK Government Foresight group on the *Tackling Obesities: Future Choices* project. Outputs from the project are available on the Foresight website: http://www.foresight.gov.uk/index.asp.

3 The new guy was probably modifying one of Issac Asimov's favourite sayings: "Violence is the last refuge of the incompetent." It was a maxim of Salvor Hardin's, a key character in Asimov's *Foundation* series.

Truth 37

1 SWOT is a strengths, weaknesses, opportunities and threats analysis. It focuses primarily on things that you control, or could control, such as resources and operational elements.

2 STEEP is an environmental analysis. It looks beyond your organisation towards things that influence you and your choices.

3 The original BCG matrix was built in 1973. The story of it can be found at http://www.bcg.com.

4 Introduced by Robert Kaplan and David Norton, in a number of articles since 1992 and in their book *The Balanced Scorecard* (1996), Harvard Business School Press.

5 Introduced by Michael Porter in 1979.

Truth 38

1 Griffin, R. Morgan (2006), Is laughter the best medicine?, *CBS News*, 7 April. http://www.cbsnews.com. See also this press

release by University of Maryland Medical Centre, Research led by Michael Miler MD, Director of Preventative Cardiology, 7 March 2005, http://www.umm.edu/news/releases/laughter2.htm.

2 *Fawlty Towers*, Episode: Communication Problems, Series 2, February 1979.

3 Sherrin, Ned (ed.) (2001), *The Oxford Dictionary of Humorous Quotations*, Oxford: Oxford University Press, p. 155.

Truth 39

1 A widely used version of Francis Bacon's phrase, "Knowledge itself is power." Knowles, Elizabeth (ed.) (1997), *The Oxford Dictionary of Phrase, Saying and Quotation*, Oxford: Oxford University Press, pp. 237–238.

2 http://www.dilbert.com/.

3 Bolchover, David (2005), *The Living Dead*, Chichester: Capstone Publishing.

Truth 40

1 Ehrlich, Eugene (1992), *Nil Desperandum: A Dictionary of Latin Tags and Phrases*, Chatham: Mackays of Chatham. This phrase—*quod cibus est allis, allis est venenum*—translates to, "What is food to some is poison to others."

Truth 42

1 More about GameChanger is available on the Shell website: http://www.shell.com/.

2 Gandhi was describing the stages of non-violent activism. According to Wikipedia, this may be a misattribution. A version of the phrase was contained in Gandhi's 1914 speech to the Amalgamated Clothing Workers of America: "And, my friends, in this story you have a history of this entire movement. First they ignore you. Then they ridicule you. And then they attack you and want to burn you. And then they build monuments to you. And that is what is going to happen to the Amalgamated Clothing Workers of America."

Truth 43

1 The company behind One Water is Global Ethics Limited, based in London. See http://www.onedifference.org/home.

2 The website is now archived, but won the Webby Award for Best Activist Site of the Year in 2007, before its closure: http://www.greenmyapple.org/.

Truth 44

1 Ohmae, Kenichi (1990), *The Borderless World*, London: William Collins & Co.

2 More detail on the X Prize Foundation can be found at http://www.xprize.org/.

Author's Acknowledgements

Much of what I have been allowed to experience, and is related in this book, has happened because of my time as Director of Creaticity at Orange. Hans Snook and Kenny Hirschhorn gave me this opportunity, for which I am grateful.

I am lucky to have worked with some wonderful people in the Imaginarium and subsequently via thoughtengine. Your stories are throughout this book. Thank you for the times that we have problem-solved together and for your continued inventiveness. Thank you to Sam Jackson at Pearson for the chance to share these stories.

Paul Coffey, Cliff Dennett and Nick Foggin have been, and continue to be, sounding boards, sources of knowledge and valued companions on this journey.

My family and friends have provided much encouragement. I will be forever grateful to Amelia for her tireless editing, as well as her belief in the project and in me. Charlotte and Oliver have been patient and supportive. They are a constant source of inspiration.

Lastly, I would like to thank the people who look after Richmond Park and the makers of Jelly Babies. Ready access to both were key to writing this book.

Publisher's Acknowledgements

We are grateful to the following for permission to reproduce copyright material:

4 lines from 'Funeral Blues', *Collected Poems*, by W.H. Auden, London: Faber and Faber Ltd.

Every effort has been made by the publisher to obtain permission from the appropriate source to reproduce material which appears in this book. In some instances we may have been unable to trace the owners of copyright material and would appreciate any information that would enable us to do so.

About the Author

Patrick Harris is the definitive blue-sky thinker, driven by an ultimate desire to reach practical, workable solutions. He is appreciated for his ability to inspire creativity in individuals, distil strategies into actionable plans and generate powerful momentum inside organisations. Much of his expertise and recognition emanates from his work as Director of Creaticity for the Orange Group. Working for the executive board, Patrick co-designed and managed the corporate strategic think tank that underpinned the company's strategy during the octane-fuelled period of 1998–2002. After leaving Orange, he founded thoughtengine, a consultancy working in numerous sectors and focusing on creativity, strategy, brand and futures. Patrick enjoys helping people and organisations to resolve complex issues and to employ inspired strategies.

He is a former non-executive Director of France Telecom UK R&D and is currently a Director of Medinge, a brand think tank focusing on furthering the humanitarian efforts of brands and their organisations—http://www.medinge.org/. Patrick is recognised as an engaging and thought-provoking speaker.

Patrick was born in the USA and complemented his early career with ten years of competitive water skiing. He holds a BSc and an MBA (Hons), is married with two children and lives in London. He can be contacted via thoughtengine—http://www.thoughtengine.co.uk/.